DECIDING TO COACH

The Mindset and Business Strategy for Aspiring Coaches

ZOE HAWKINS & JO WHEATLEY

authors
AND CO.

CONTENTS

DEDICATIONS

Zoe - To my husband Ben – I am forever thankful for you and your unwavering support. These dreams are made all the more possible with you sharing them with me. To our children, you are always enough, in every way. Lastly, to my Mum, you've always enabled me to chase my dreams and you continue to do that in so many ways today – not least the childcare!

Jo – To my husband, children and parents, thank you for being my rock and having whole hearted belief in everything I do. You enable me to support so many others and have taught me so much. Your heart is my heart.

Thank you to our coaching tutors, supervisors and clients who have shared and contributed to our journey. We are forever grateful for the wisdom of our conversations and the safe spaces to learn and grow together.

This book is also dedicated to you as a compassionate and courageous leader, whose whole person approach to relationships is changing the world for the better, supporting everyday mental health.

ABOUT THE AUTHORS

Jo Wheatley (left) & Zoe Hawkins (right)

Welcome to 'Deciding to Coach'. We are Jo Wheatley and Zoe Hawkins, master accredited coaches, triple accredited coach trainers, qualified and experienced coach supervisors, mums, wives and friends. We are founders of the global coaching training organisation, In Good Company (www.igcompany. co.uk) and of the online coaching community and number 1 podcast, 'The Coaching Crowd'.

We met at university when we were working in our Human Resources careers and began our Masters in Personnel and Development. We've always enjoyed learning and so it seems fitting that we met in this way. Coaching was something that came onto our radar after we met, and it came into more focus and impact when we were coached ourselves in our HR leadership roles. After experiencing it, we knew we needed to learn more about it. Experiencing coaching enabled us to build our confidence, clarify our purpose and discover our mission to change conversations and ignite more compassion and courage in everyday leadership, thereby improving mental health for all. For us, this is the missing piece of leadership, the part that's essential for wellbeing at scale, as well as strategic progression. We fell in love with positively impacting lives through coaching and decided to make it our full-time career.

In 2011 we set up In Good Company, our coaching business, providing executive coaching, coaching workshops and leadership development programmes underpinned by coaching psychology. In 2015 we began training coaches on our accredited training programmes and today, In Good Company has become a globally accredited coaching training business. We train coaches all over the world through our triple accredited, award nominated, coaching qualifications. We are award winning and multi award nominated master accredited coaches, and we've coached leaders across a wide range of industries across the globe. This includes individual contributors, first line managers, through to board members of global organisations.

Today, our business has a global impact and continues to grow at pace. More importantly, we've created a thriving community of coaches and aspiring coaches in our Coaching Crowd community on Facebook, in our Coaching Crowd Business Lounge membership and on our popular You Tube Channel, where we share free coaching resources with our communities. Our Coaching Crowd Podcast helps people to understand the power of coaching and explore how they can use it in their lives and career. It went to Number 1 in the Apple Careers Charts and Number 4 in the Apple Business Charts and ranked in the top 1.5% of all podcasts globally. We have always had a desire to add value and enable as many people as possible to access high quality, ethical coaching knowledge and resources, removing financial barriers as much as possible and now, we're able to bring you our professional coaching expertise and training to help you decide how to move on from the crossroads you're at in this book.

We're proud to be female leaders. We've built a business from the ground up and we've done all of that whilst raising our children and living busy family lives. We are female CEO's, living in our forever homes on the coast, working every day to help people be the best they can be, whilst training others as coaches so they can build a career they can be proud of and have a greater positive impact. It could have remained a dream, but we created a plan, designed the life we wanted to live and took the steps to get us there. We want to help you design the life you want to achieve and work out the steps to get you there too.

Here's a bit about our individual stories in transitioning to a career in coaching:

Jo's Story:

I was always fascinated by psychology, wanting to understand the way people think. When I discovered coaching and worked with a coach, I felt a sense of coming home. Everything about coaching aligned to feedback I'd received about my strengths. I set a goal to find a training provider who would cover the depths of psychology and when I found them, I knew it was right for me.

My goal to train as a coach was to deepen skills that would help me achieve whichever career choice I made next. As I trained as a coach, I discovered my values, overcame limiting beliefs and I developed a confidence around coaching as a career. I wasn't planning to leave my HR role at that point, but I had to make a decision about whether I wanted to continue on a CEO pathway.

I made the decision to leave my corporate career part way through my course. I had a young child and my husband was working abroad 50% of the time. I had the support of my parents and I set the goal of working for myself. When I spoke to Zoe about my plans, we set a goal together to create our own coaching and leadership development business. Making the decision to train as a coach was the single best career decision I ever made and has enabled me to achieve subsequent goals I didn't even think were possible at that point.

The goal to write a book came way before training as a coach, after I was given feedback at school about how I should be an author. To realise that goal in this book has been rewarding and has taught me so much.

Achieving my goals in a values aligned way has been totally fulfilling. When my time is up in this world, I and those who love and care for me will know that I designed and lived my life in accordance with the things that matter most to me, including creating a positive legacy for others, and I felt satisfied everyday with the goals I set and achieved.

Zoe's story

I've always been determined and strong-willed. Once I get an idea in my head and I commit to it, I see it through. Finding coaching gave me a channel for this. I discovered that I could live my life by design. Knowing what is deeply important to me, what I need to be fulfilled and having the skills to set goals that I am in control of enables me to bypass self-doubt and fear, in order to focus on the actions I can take to bring me more joy and ease.

I decided to train as a coach at a point in my life when my career was going well and I enjoyed what I did. I'd always wanted my own business and the more my career progressed, the less I could shake off the urge. I chose to invest in coaching training because I was fascinated by it. Although I had an intention to set up in business at some point in the future, I didn't 100% believe that I'd leave my corporate job and become a coach. However, I did know that when the time came to take the leap, I needed to be ready, and the coaching training would help me.

My window of opportunity came about a year after I'd qualified as a coach, when I was pregnant with my first child and my husband was deployed to Afghanistan. I knew I didn't want to juggle an international career with looking after my daughter. I wanted to be there for my new family, and so one of us would need to dramatically change their career to align to that. I felt it was time for me to find the courage and set up in business as a coach. This career path would enable me to have more freedom which, with a young child, is what I wanted. I was still nervous, and reluctant to leave the security of a stable corporate career, but I could also see this was my time. So, I took a deep breath and went all in with becoming a coach, and it was the single best decision I have ever made for my career.

Had I never taken those first steps to train as a coach, I would not have been ready to seize the opportunity presented to me. Never underestimate the importance of getting started when you don't have all the answers. Needing all the answers is a fear response and a form of self sabotage. Getting started, taking the next obvious step is something we are all in control of.

If you have discovered us for the first time in this book, welcome. We are delighted you've joined us.

HOW TO MAKE THE MOST OF THIS BOOK

This book contains two distinct parts.

The first part is all about your decision making and whilst each chapter has its own distinct focus, each chapter echoes the others as the concepts are interrelated and will enable you to embed the learning.

The second part of the book is all about setting up a successful and sustainable coaching business, so you have full knowledge of what's involved in building and running a coaching business. We share with you the model that has bought us success and one that we see working in the industry. Our aim is that in knowing what's involved, you will feel fully equipped to make a confident decision about whether or not you'll decide to coach.

Throughout the book, there are coaching activities, so we encourage you to have resources ready to capture your answers as you go. All of this content will support you in your decision to coach.

Each chapter also has a summary at the end which contains the key learnings from the chapter, along with a few reflection questions. Reflective practice is the foundation of professional and personal development and is a core coaching competency that enables you to make new connections, therefore giving you more choices.

You may choose to read this book in one go, chapter by chapter, or perhaps in two separate parts. It is designed as a book to help you make the decision about coaching, as well as the design of your coaching business. It is a book you may be drawn back to time and time again as you take each step, and one that you can dip into chapters of as you work through each step. Whichever way you engage with it, know that we wrote this for you.

Part One

DECIDING TO COACH: THE MINDSET

> "Making the best decision for you with certainty and confidence requires you to lean into your beliefs, the core of what's important to you and your identity. It requires a deep knowledge and understanding of who you are."

- JOANNE WHEATLEY & ZOE HAWKINS

PURPOSE

E verything in a life is a decision. When you have a growing sense that change is needed in your life, it grows. Ignoring it doesn't make it go away. You're not alone, every single person that comes to coaching is struggling with their decision making and asking themselves questions like " how will I know if this is the right decision for me?". The reality is, when you're asking yourself questions like these, change is already happening. You're either going to decide to stay as you are, or you're going to decide to make changes, and we know that what you really need is to check with your internal compass and gain the confidence to fully embrace what you probably already know.

Living our purpose in life requires decision making at significant points in our life. It sounds easy, but decision making is emotional and trusting ourselves as resourceful and capable of making decisions is key. The fact that you're reading this book, "Deciding to Coach" tells you there's a decision inside of you waiting to be made. This book is going to help you to decide with confidence if coaching is the next ambitious career move for you. It's also about learning how to make decisions, because every decision we make sparks a ripple effect. Deciding whether or not to become a coach is just the first decision in a string of decisions that you're making for your career.

On the surface decision making seems easy; we are taught to write a pros and cons list and as long as the pros outweigh the cons, people would say go for it. But in reality, making the best decision for you with certainty and confidence requires you to lean into your beliefs, the core of what's important to you and your identity. It requires a deep knowledge and understanding of who you are.

Time is precious and it's so easy for months or even years to go by, living with a thought and not actually translating it into action. You can get paralysed by the fear of making the wrong decision and get stuck, not fulfilling your purpose in life. Sometimes the fear is about succeeding and everything that may change as a result of that, and sometimes the fear is about wanting something so passionately and facing the pain of disappointment if it doesn't work out.

Indecisiveness, in a mild form, is a nuisance, however, when it comes to things that really matter, indecisiveness is corrosive to your wellbeing. You might lose sleep, your comfort zone shrinks, it eats away at your confidence, and you end up with Groundhog Day. It's not just you it affects; when you're feeling confused and you're tired of churning the same thoughts over and over in your mind, you feel frustrated and probably get short tempered, meaning others around you are affected too. Decisiveness is underrated.

It's not decision making that people find hard, it's what the decision may mean, or perhaps the uncertainty of what the decision will lead to. For you to be able to make your decisions confidently and courageously, it's going to require you to journey into yourself and that's exactly what we're going to do in this book. So, if you've ever been told "you'd make a great coach" and found yourself wondering if that could be a great career move, then you're in the right place.

It's a significant decision to leave your employed role behind and make a career pivot to follow your purpose and train as a coach. It can feel exciting and terrifying all at the same time. On the one hand, staying where you are doesn't really feel like an option, but on the other hand, deciding to go all in and follow your purpose feels daunting too. You're not alone at this crossroads. It's normal to want more impact, and to leave a positive and notable legacy, with the ability to make a wholehearted difference in the world.

Many people that decide to coach have ticked so many boxes in their career. To the outside world, they have it all – secure work, decent salary, peers and colleagues to socialise with, promising career prospects, but internally there's a conflict, a longing for more impact and meaning. What starts as a niggle of doubt about what the future holds for their career, becomes a much louder distraction and reaches a point where they can't shake the feeling that they're not as fulfilled as they want to be and as high achievers, that doesn't sit comfortably. Does this resonate with you? Perhaps you love helping others and get so much joy from supporting people to learn and grow; it's a point on the compass that you keep being drawn to follow. Maybe, you want to contribute to creating a shift in the world, an awakening where relationships are deeper, more meaningful and where they facilitate growth, alignment and wellbeing. Is your soul calling for more?

Do achievement, ambition, drive, meaning and purpose run through your veins? Do you suspect you won't be satisfied until you can meet this need inside of you? Is there a whisper inside of you that tells you you're playing small in terms of what's possible for you? As you learn to accept all parts of yourself and honour your desire for more impact and meaning, deciding to coach can become easy.

The part of deciding to coach that can be hard is within the hidden part of you. The part of you that's apprehensive to share these thoughts publicly for fear of what others will think and how you'll be judged. When a bold vision comes into your mind your internal saboteur voice says "Can I really do that?......What will everyone think? Do I really have it in me? What if I fail? Is this really me?". So many doubts and fears can get in the way of bringing your ambitions to life, but those thoughts are not facts, they are simply limiting beliefs. As much as there is a side to you that is doubtful, there is also a confident, ambitious side of you too. As a tenacious, high achiever, you know you can succeed, it's just a case of deciding wholeheartedly what you want and need, then you can make a plan, follow the steps and be the change you want to see. Clarity is the key to your inner confidence.

By now, you might be thinking yes, but even if I decided I did want to become a coach, how would I leave my employed role and actually make that happen? This book is going to cover that too, because we know when people decide to coach, they like to go in with their eye's wide open.

To become a successful coach, you need to have experienced coaching yourself and also train to become a qualified and accredited coach. So, in this book we'll take you through key coaching topics and help you to:

- Understand what coaching is and the realities of working as a coach
- Decide whether you would make a great coach and if it will satisfy your desire for more impact
- Explore how being a coach honours your values
- Identify and overcome limiting beliefs you have that may be holding you back from taking the critical steps forward
- Help you identify how to choose the right coach training provider for you
- Demystify the coaching world

- Find out how you can transition from your employed role into coaching
- Build a plan so you can take your first steps to making change in your career

By reading this book we'll help you to see that there is a truly fulfilling life beyond being an employee, where your career trajectory and your credibility can soar beyond the constraints of your existing role. We'll share with you our knowledge of what makes an award winning, master accredited coach, how to know if coaching could be a great fit for your talents and how to set up a successful and sustainable coaching business. We peel back the layers of the coaching industry and share our knowledge with you - all the things we would have found useful when we were where you are now.

As you work through this book, you'll move through the confusion and uncertainty and gain clarity, learning that you are your own solution. As you nurture the skills to coach yourself, and become confident in your decision making, you'll realise the transformative power of coaching. At the end of the book, you'll be informed and ready to take on the next chapter of your career as a change maker and legacy creator. Imagine what that will do for your wellbeing.

Whether you end up deciding to coach or not, you'll leave this book having gained peace of mind and be able to recognise what's deeply important to you in life and in work. You'll build confidence and connection to voice that bold, courageous leader inside of you and feel empowered to make your whispered dreams a reality. The world needs you to fulfil your purpose and you'll be able to do all of that with pride, focus and tenacity.

REFLECTION QUESTIONS

As we draw this chapter to a close, let's finish with some questions for you to reflect on to help you connect to your purpose:

What's the best decision you've ever made for yourself?

What do you need to fully trust yourself?

What conditions need to be in place for you to make decisions confidently?

CHAPTER SUMMARY

The key learning points from this chapter include:

1. Decision making is emotional and trusting ourselves as resourceful and capable of making decisions is key.
2. Making the best decision for you with certainty and confidence requires you to lean into your beliefs, the core of what's important to you and your identity. It requires a deep knowledge and understanding of who you are.
3. Deciding to coach is about living a life and having a career that is more than a salary. It's about your legacy.

WHAT IS COACHING?

> *"Coaching is about creating safe spaces where people can bring their whole, authentic selves and be fully accepted"*
>
> — *JO WHEATLEY & ZOE HAWKINS*

E very good decision you make begins with you being able to coach yourself and be knowledgeable about the topic. The coaching industry has developed significantly as a profession since it's inception in the 1980s and continues to evolve rapidly to meet the emerging needs of today and tomorrow. There is huge scope to contribute to its development as there are many different specialisms within the coaching industry. In this chapter, we'll start by helping you to fully understand the coaching industry, demystifying what coaching is and what makes coaching different to everyday conversations.

There are professional bodies that provide structure and informal regulation to the industry. Ethical coaches use the coaching bodies to guide their professional development and demonstrate their commitment to quality. The three main bodies for the coaching industry are The European Mentoring and Coaching Council (EMCC), The International Coach Federation (ICF) and the Association for Coaching (AC).

The coaching bodies provide accreditation, which qualified coaches can apply for. There are different levels of accreditation to reflect the levels of experience and training qualified coaches have. So, step one for someone who wants to become a coach is to undertake a coaching training that is accredited by one of the coaching bodies and then, after achieving the coaching qualification, the coach applies to their chosen body for individual accreditation.

Although they are separate, independent bodies, they have similar code of ethics and are committed to raising the standards of the coaching profession. Each of the coaching bodies have their own core coaching competency frameworks and provide accreditation pathways for coaches to demonstrate their experience and expertise.

The International Coach Federation define coaching as "partnering with clients in a thought-provoking and creative process that inspires them to maximize their personal and professional potential, which is particularly important in today's uncertain and complex environment".[1]

The European Mentoring and Coaching Council define Coaching and Mentoring as "a professionally guided process that inspires clients to maximise their personal and professional potential. It is a structured, purposeful and transformational process, helping clients to see and test alternative ways for improvement of competence, decision making and enhancement of quality of life. Coach and Mentor and client work together in a partnering relationship on strictly confidential terms. In this relationship, clients are experts on the content and decision making level; the coach and mentor is an expert in professionally guiding the process".[2]

Put simply, coaching is a process that enables someone to progress from where they are in their life now, to where they want to be. At it's core, coaching is about change. It's about enabling someone to fully understand their current situation, identify the small or significant change(s) they want to make and work to understand and close the gap that is stopping them from getting there. The purpose of coaching is discovery, awareness, choice, learning and a space for safe exploration.

Coaching is…

- A learnable skill
- Highly effective
- A process
- Values driven
- Both formal and ad hoc
- A choice
- Proactive
- Useful in groups and teams

The role of a coach is defined by the EMCC as "an expert in establishing a relationship with people in a series of conversations with the purpose of:

- Serving the clients to improve their performance or enhance their personal development or both, choosing their own goals and ways of doing it
- Interacting with each person or group by applying one or more relevant methods, according to standards and ethical principles set up by EMCC and other professional associations".[3]

Another way to think of the coach is as a facilitator of the coaching process, which supports the client to set and achieve goals that are well formed. A coach supports their client to coach themselves and provides a kind of support that is distinct from any other, with a level of presence, listening and unconditional acceptance that you will rarely experience elsewhere. A coach is an objective and compassionate thought, emotions and reflective partner.

Coaching is unique because coaches believe that their clients have all of the answers within themselves, and they enable the client to see different perspectives and connect with those answers – the breakthroughs. They do this by asking provocative questions, listening to ignite insight in the client, rather than respond from their own ego, sharing observations and feedback and facilitating coaching activities. Their role is to enable the client to find answers for themselves.

There is so much more depth to coaching and the role of a coach than any simple definition can capture. For us, coaching is about creating safe spaces where people can bring their whole, authentic selves and be fully accepted. It's a place where they can realign their thinking, feeling and actions to design and achieve their best life. It's a courageous and compassionate space where support and challenge are balanced and clients experience the full, contactful presence of another, holding space for them.

The depth to coaching comes when we introduce the complexity of human behaviour and how our minds work with our conscious and unconscious mind. Our conscious mind is our decision making one. It's the one that decides what we'll have for breakfast, whether we're going to stop for coffee, what email to action first. It's the part of our mind that sets our goals, and it plays an important role in coaching. Think of it as the goal setter.

Its partner is the unconscious mind. The goal getter. Our unconscious mind dictates how we experience the world. When we are in any situation, we run the information we receive from our senses (what we see, hear, feel, smell and taste) through our filters (our values, beliefs, attitudes, decision making strategies, personality preferences and previous life experiences) in order to make sense of what is happening moment by moment. Our unconscious mind is where our memories are stored and where our emotions reside. It draws down information when we need it. Think of it like a software programme running in the back of your mind where it's always at work, busy trying to get our unconscious needs met.

There can be a barrier between the conscious and unconscious mind, called the critical faculty, which can mean that the flow of information is interrupted. When this happens, we can experience a feeling of misalignment, tension, inner conflict or resistance. Coaching can help to reconnect the two by helping the client to increase their awareness of the interaction between the two, so that they have more choice, and it's from having choice that they can create change.

Coaching conversations are different from general conversations in another way, as it is a relationship that is contracted for, which means it involves permission and agreement about commitments, boundaries and expectations. There is a natural curiosity about the difference between coaching, mentoring, therapy and consulting. There are boundaries between these, as well as overlaps. If we take coaching and mentoring and imagine them on a continuum; coaching at one end and mentoring at the other. Mentoring in its purest form is directive – advice giving. Coaching at the other end, in its purest form, is non directive, meaning the coach only asks clean questions. In reality, coaches will move around the continuum. What's important is the need to be aware of where they are on the continuum at every point in the conversation and make conscious choices about how best to be in service of their client, based on the contract.

Mentoring is typically where a more experienced person shares their wisdom, guidance and advice with someone who has less experience than them and it's often centred around a topic, such as career growth. There are other forms of mentoring too, such as reverse mentoring where someone with less experience may mentor someone with more experience - for example, a new starter sharing their experiences on joining an organisation with a senior leader who is working to improve onboarding processes.

Great mentors use coaching skills when supporting mentees. The main difference from coaching is that a mentor is seen as the person who has the answers, whereas in coaching, the coach sees that the client holds the answer. Or can find the answer.

The difference between coaching and therapy is another boundary that needs managing in coaching. Therapy is support that is often sought at a time of crisis, when the problem or struggle that the client is experiencing may be affecting every aspect of their lives. Clients that seek therapy are often having a response to trauma. This may be trauma that has been recently experienced, or trauma that has been experienced in the past and is now triggered and affecting them in their life today. This type of support is approached by exploring the past, in order to better understand the current challenge. Therapy helps a client to understand their trauma response. By understanding the challenge, it provides the client with more options and helps them to feel more in control and rebuild.

The similarities are that both coaching and therapy promote a deeper understanding, yet the approach therapy takes is to do this from exploring past experiences to learn how to thrive and function in the present. In coaching the past may be explored but only in so much as it is relevant to the goals that the client has set, and coaching has a more direct focus on goals and moving into the future, rather than learning how to regain stability in the present.

Consultancy is another approach that can get confused with coaching. Consultants are experts on a niche topic, brought into an organisation to share their expertise to resolve a specific problem, often using tried and tested processes. Whilst many consultants may use coaching skills to help to bring people on board to their ideas and concepts, consulting is more of a 'tell' approach. Organisations who invest in consulting are looking for others to solve challenges or problems that exist in their organisation.

Coaching is very different to this. Coaches don't need to be experts in the role their clients have. It's very possible for a coach who has no experience of the technology sector to work with a senior leader in technology for example. Sometimes it can be helpful for a coach to have no prior knowledge of the role or sector their client works in because it means they can be wholly objective. Coaches are experts in coaching tools, techniques and mindset. Often when coaches start out, they can feel intimidated coaching people who are in roles more senior to any they have held, but they soon realise that their role and value is in the relationship and their coaching skills, which are critical for that individual's success. Coaching is a 'do with' relationship, not 'do to'. We think of it as a co-created, learning relationship. If a client perceives their coach to be in a 'one up' position in some way, then it's easy for the client to assume that the coach holds the power, this limits the client's ability to discover the answers for themselves. Empowerment comes from equality. A clear difference between coaching and consulting is that the coach confers power to the coaching relationship because they know they are not the expert in the client's problem – even if they have experienced this problem themselves.

Like all other approaches, the reality is that many clients like their coaches to have some experience or understanding of the world they work in, and so you'll find many organisations engaging with coaches that have backgrounds in their industry. Many coaches like to have an understanding of their clients' world and often choose to niche down into areas where they have lived experience, for example, there are coaches supporting ex-pats, coaches supporting clients with divorce, as well as coaches who support with career transition and confidence.

In coaching, we learn early on to see all client challenges as unique and novel. Our own experiences of these problems can't be the same as our clients because we all experience the world differently. This is often the part of the learning journey that trainee coaches find difficult, but incredibly rewarding. The journey involves moving away from the need to rescue and instead, see each person as whole and resourceful. Coaches learn that in rescuing someone, we can inadvertently position them as a victim, even when they hadn't seen or experienced themselves in that way before. The ethos of coaching is about empowerment.

Understanding what coaching is, and what coaching isn't, the next natural question is "could I be a coach?". The answer is yes. We all have coaching capability. We are born with an innate desire to learn and grow. Our life experiences shape us into who we are today and how we experience the world. We make decisions on a daily basis that are influenced by our unconscious thoughts and most of the time, we believe we are in control of those decisions. The fact that you're sitting here reading this book, enquiring about whether there is a more fulfilling career possible for you, is proof that your inner coach is at work. Your unconscious mind is searching for answers, leading you here.

The only difference between you and us is that you haven't learnt how to make the most of your internal coach yet. As you learn to coach yourself, you will see how powerful and possible it is that you can create a wildly fulfilling career out of helping others to do the same.

REFLECTION QUESTIONS

As we draw this chapter to a close, let's finish with some questions for you to reflect on to help you define your relationship to coaching as a profession:

What excites me about coaching?

What am I thinking now about a career as a coach?

What questions have I answered?

CHAPTER SUMMARY

The key learning points from this chapter include:

1. Coaches believe that the answers lie within their clients and by using skills such as questioning, listening, observation and feedback they ignite new perspectives and awareness in their clients that enable them to see new choices and take actions that create change.
2. Coaching is different to mentoring, therapy and consulting. A core principle of coaching is that it's about equality. The coach does not know better than the client, they are not the expert. Equality conveys power to the relationship.
3. You are your own coach and are always coaching yourself. The only difference between you and other coaches is that you haven't yet learned how to use your natural, innate ability in a conscious way.

STRENGTHS

" *Strengths are those things that you find so easy you almost take them for granted, but when you take time to acknowledge, understand and appreciate your strengths they are the gateway to a completely fulfilling career* "

— *ZOE HAWKINS AND JO WHEATLEY*

I t takes strength to make the best decision for you. If it was easy, you'd have already made the decision and actioned it. Strength comes from knowing your unique talents and making decisions that are in alignment with them. Now that you have clarity on what coaching is, we'll help you explore how your strengths align to the role of a coach and we'll begin by defining what strengths are.

Our strengths are the sweet spot between what we do naturally and easily and also what we enjoy. These are often the things other people always comment on us doing so well, but that we often discount as it is so natural for us. It's important to identify your strengths because once you know what you're good at – your zone of genius – you can begin to orientate yourself to what brings you energy and enjoyment. Pause for a moment and consider what strengths you're using when people ask you "how do you do that?"

When we lean into our strengths, we find high levels of achievement and enjoyment coexisting. One without the other isn't fulfilling. Investing in a career where we get to leverage our strengths and be rewarded for them brings us satisfaction, as well as a sensation of working in flow.

People often find themselves in careers which they are really good at, but they don't enjoy and it leaves them feeling empty. This is often the point when they reach out for a coach because it's confusing. At school, we're often taught to pursue simply what we are good at, but this is one dimensional and ignores all the life experiences and resources we gain as we grow up. The focus needs to be identifying the cross section of your talents and what you enjoy. It is where your purpose ignites joy.

We collect labels through our life and our experiences at work. Labels can lead us to perceive our strengths as something that we 'shouldn't' have and in coaching, we often help clients to peel back the layers which have led to people burying or hiding their true talents. For example, you may get labelled as "sensitive" from an early age because your emotions are visible to others and you are highly empathic. You may come to associate this as a bad thing and do your best to cover up this 'sensitive' quality. Labels are not helpful because they are not the truth, they are other peoples' perceptions and opinions. Being sensitive can enable you to connect with people and understand them at a deep level. It can be an incredible skill for team building, networking and of course, coaching!

A further challenge that is often experienced in employed roles is adapting to fit in. In work, you might perceive that certain skills or behaviours are valued more and you work hard to adopt the 'model' of behaviour and talent that is recognised. In doing so, it can help you to progress your career, but if our natural skills, talents and ways of being aren't aligned to the organisation's, you dim your light (your strengths) by moving further and further away from your purpose. No one wants that, but it can happen easily. Let's pause and consider: How aligned is your current role to your talents? Does your role or organisational culture require you to dim your light? Do you want to find a place where you can shine bright as a beacon of hope and belonging for yourself and for others?

Coaches enable people to identify their strengths and use them to achieve their goals. Many traditional approaches to personal and professional development focus on weaknesses and closing the gap, and whilst it can be helpful to grow in areas where we lack strength, it is possible to make progress when you focus on what you are already good at and learn to leverage your strengths to help you in areas where you are less strong. It takes a lot of energy to become excellent at something that isn't in your zone of genius, so as coaches, we help clients to reconnect with what they are naturally good at and free themselves from the expectation that they need to be excellent at everything.

Let's focus on you. What are you recognised for? What is easy for you and difficult for others? What do you love? What are you proud of having achieved? Take five minutes to write down your top 10 strengths. Think about when you are in flow, what are you doing?

It is sometimes easier for others to identify strengths in you. Zoe will tell you that one of Jo's strengths is researching and Jo will share with you that one of Zoe's strengths is tenacity. Other strengths we share and see in each other, as well as receiving feedback from clients on, are an incredible ability to learn rapidly and enjoy the process of learning, to relate to others – building intimacy quickly in relationships. We see patterns and make connections between things easily. We are strategists - we identify a goal that aligns to our values and drive forward. Do you share any of these strengths?

When you know what your strengths are, you can use them to bridge the gap between where you are now and where you want to be. For example, perhaps right now you're not using all of your strengths, or they aren't fully appreciated. As you recognise and embrace your strengths, you'll begin to realise that they don't have to be squished or dimmed to fit in. Instead, you can use those strengths to guide you to a role where your strengths can be fully used and therefore enjoy success on a greater, more aligned scale. This is what it is to maximise your potential.

As you're considering a career in coaching, we'll introduce you to core coaching competencies so you can see how your strengths and talents fit within this role. Coaching bodies seek to raise the standards of the profession of coaching and one of the ways they do this is by providing competency frameworks for coaches to use. Each coaching body has their own competency framework. They're all very similar. Aligning to a set of core competencies provides a framework for growth and helps you to gain a deeper understanding of the coaching profession. Here, we'll share with you the eight core competencies from the EMCC, each with a reflection question for you. They are:

1. Understanding Self

This is about your awareness of own values, beliefs and behaviour, and your ability to recognise how these affect your coaching practice. Self-awareness is important in being able to know how you'll meet your client's objectives. You also need to be able to notice if and when you are triggered by something in a coaching session and learn from these experiences.

Reflection for you – Do you enjoy learning about yourself and reflecting on experiences you have had? Are you fascinated by what and how you think? If so, this is a competency that may be a good fit for you.

2. Commitment To Self-Development

This is about your commitment to continually learn and grow to be the best coach that you can be. It is about being an ethical coach and maintaining the standards and reputation of the profession. As coaches, we are lifelong learners. The learner mindset enables us to co-create the learning space which is an important part of coaching conversations.

Reflection for you – Do you enjoy continued professional development and stretching your skills and strengths? Are you always looking for interesting courses and resources, wanting to stimulate new perspectives and insights? If so, this may be something you'd enjoy about the coaching profession and a great competency fit for you.

3. Managing The Contract

This is about how you manage the relationship and agenda you set with your client. When you manage the contract, you create and maintain expectations and boundaries of the coaching contract with the client and, where appropriate, with sponsors. When we say contract, this is both the psychological contract and the practical elements of coaching. Managing the contract is about creating a safe space for your client and reassuring them about confidentiality. It's about making sure that the coaching is appropriate to their needs and learning styles. As a coach, we need to be adaptable and pay attention to our clients' needs at all times. It takes courage and discipline.

Reflection for you – Do you enjoy understanding the needs of others? Are you good at negotiating a personalized way of working? If so, this may be a good sign that you'd manage contracts well in coaching.

4. Building The Relationship

This is a competency at the centre of coaching. It's about skillfully building and maintaining an effective relationship with the client, using skills such as rapport building, empathy and deep listening to build trust and a transformational space. It is also about being attuned to relational needs. Coaching relationships are high in trust and as the coach, you confer power to the relationship by approaching your client as an equal and believing in their ability to help themselves.

Reflection for you – What do you enjoy about relationship building? Do you enjoy creating deep, meaningful relationships? If so, you are likely to have a strength in this competency.

5. Enabling Insight And Learning

This is how you use your skills to empower your client. Your role is to ignite your clients thinking and facilitate breakthroughs, enabling them to gain fresh new insights which gives them additional choices and growth. In coaching, you'll do this by using your skills in listening and questioning as well as using tools and techniques. Enabling insight and learning is how you bring together all the of your skills and competencies in service of your client. It's often about using your intuition and making good judgements about what to do and when in a coaching conversation.

Reflection for you – Are you skilled in facilitating people to connect with new insight and learning? Is this what you enjoy most in your role? Do you want to do more of this? If so, this may be a strength for you.

6. Outcome And Action Orientation

Action is an important part of coaching because it's how the client moves forward and achieves their goals. It's a core part of coaching that differentiates it from other forms of support. In coaching we support clients to set actions that take them towards the outcomes they are looking for. This can often involve challenging clients to aim higher and supporting them to overcome reservations or obstacles they perceive to taking those actions.

Reflection for you – Do you enjoy helping people to set actions and plan for the future? Do you find this is a natural focus for your conversations? If so, you are likely to find this competency a strength.

7. Use Of Models And Techniques

Coaches share models and use coaching techniques to facilitate the change that the client wants to achieve. These models enable a client to gain new perspectives and empower them. It also educates their inner coach so they can support themselves long after the coaching relationship ends. Many clients also take what they have learned through their own coaching experience to pay the coaching forward and help others.

Reflection for you – Do you enjoy psychology and theoretical models and sharing them to help people learn? Are you someone who is curious about how things work? Are you creative and like to create your own approaches to things? If so, using models and techniques could be a strength for you.

8. Evaluation

This is about how you gather information on the effectiveness of your practice. It provides content for your own reflections and continuous development plan. It also enables you to collate evidence to demonstrate the value of coaching and how you receive recognition for your efforts and model a learner mindset.

Reflection for you – Do you enjoy receiving feedback and knowing the difference your work has had? Do you enjoy finding ways to demonstrate value? If so, this could be a strength for you.

Now that you've read and understand more about the EMCC competencies, score yourself out of ten on how competent and confident you feel with each of the core competencies.

We'd expect there to be some gaps as you aren't a trained coach yet. Know that no-one starts from zero when they train as a coach. Everyone brings skills and talents to the table. A coaching qualification helps to sharpen, broaden and deepen these skills through additional knowledge of evidence-based practices. Think of it as going from good to great.

REFLECTION QUESTIONS

As we draw this chapter to a close, let's finish with some questions for you to reflect on your strengths and how they align to coaching:

Which of the core competencies are you most comfortable with right now?

What are your areas for growth with coaching?

CHAPTER SUMMARY

The key learning points from this chapter include:

1. Strengths are things we're so good at that we often don't recognise them as strengths.
2. Working with our strengths brings us joy and fulfilment but often, we mould and adapt ourselves so that we no longer embrace all our talents.
3. Reconnecting with our strengths helps us to find ways to build more joy into our work.
4. The coaching profession provides competency frameworks which can help me to understand how my strengths fit into the role of a coach.

VALUES

> "*Values are your compass in life. They give you certainty in those moments when everything else might feel uncertain*"
>
> — *JO WHEATLEY & ZOE HAWKINS*

You can't make a great decision without knowing what your values are because your values are the things you must have in your life to feel fulfilled. Therefore, the next step in deciding to coach is to identify your career values and use them as a checklist to decide if a career in coaching would honour them. In this chapter, we'll guide you through what values are, why they are important and how to identify yours.

Let's start with what values are. Values are your compass in life. Knowing your values is critical to taking the steps forward that are right for you. We all have values, yet most people live their lives unaware of them because they reside in the unconscious mind. They are the source of our purest motivation.

Discovering our values changed the direction of our lives and has been the most influential thing we've learned in our journey to becoming coaches. Like you, we were once at the crossroads deciding which direction to take in our careers, wondering whether to keep going in our HR careers, perhaps pursuing a CEO role, or to specialise in what we were really drawn to, which was supporting others through coaching. Identifying our own personal career values gave us clarity, confidence and certainty about the right decision for us. That's the impact identifying values can have for everyone.

Once you have clarity on your values, you can begin truly aligning and up levelling your life with confidence. Decision making becomes easy because you know what motivates you, and you experience more joy and ease. Identifying your values is a pivotal point in your life and put simply, values give you a roadmap for your life.

Values are also how you judge right or wrong and they influence your emotions. When your values are being met you feel emotions such as fulfilment, contentment, ease and flow, whereas when your values are unmet, you can experience boredom, frustration or even anger and resentment.

Your emotions give you clues about values that may have been honoured or betrayed. Let's think about this in the work context – if you have a value around fairness and you see someone being bullied, you'll likely find yourself stepping in as your fairness value would be activated and you'll feel compelled to act, even if you are normally quite shy or reserved. You may notice that you feel a disproportionate amount of rage – as if the event is happening to you. This is because values are the things you are motivated by. They are the things you move towards or away from.

You are driven by your values and because they are often unknown to you, they are a huge source of untapped potential. Living your life in alignment with your values brings clarity, fulfilment, peace of mind, purpose and authentic success.

Values are your core needs. The things we must have in your life to support our wellbeing. Examples include security, belonging and freedom. You may be wondering what values coaches have and whether your values are aligned. Here are some of the values we see amongst successful coaches:

- Growth
- Learning
- Achievement
- Independence
- Connection
- Equality
- Helping others

Do any of these resonate with you? We understand that a part of you may be a little unsure if you've never done any work on identifying your values, so we'll guide you through an activity now to help you get clear on your values.

You can discover your career values by answering the questions below in turn. We suggest that you keep these handy so you can refer back to them when you need to. Make sure you are in a space where you are not going to be interrupted and you feel relaxed and comfortable.

Firstly, really connect with "what is essential for you to have in your career?". Write down what comes to mind, word for word. Keep connecting with those things and writing them down in a list. Ask yourself what else is important to you about your career. Take your time, ask your unconscious mind, listen to your internal voice. Allow whatever wants to come up and be heard get your attention. It's important to you. Note it down. Make sure you don't filter your responses because of what you think is or isn't acceptable. If the word 'power' pops into your head, write it down. No editing!

By now, you will have a list of at least six words or phrases. You may have fifteen. It doesn't matter. This is unique to you. It's your values DNA. There's no right or wrong or any judgement. There is your truth, and we are helping you to get closer to it. Ask yourself again "what else – what else is essential for you in your career?". Pause and note that down.

How do you feel looking at your list of things that are important to you in your career? What does that tell you? Are there any surprises in there for you?

Let's move onto the next step. This time, recall at least two events related to your career where you felt really motivated and engaged. We're looking for specific events here such as a project you led which you really enjoyed, or a presentation you delivered that went really well, or perhaps it was when you were at school, thinking about the career you were focused on? Take a moment to find two events where you were really motivated and engaged at work and write these down.

Once you have those, ask yourself, "what was it about that event that gave you that sense of motivation and engagement?". Continue to reflect. What else was important to you about that time? Go as deep as you can, keep asking yourself these questions and add any words that come up for you to your list.

It may be a time when you were excited about your career. That would tell you that excitement is probably a career value and can be added to your list. It may be that you were in a team where there was real trust, or connection, or fun. Whatever words come up, capture them – they are important to you.

The next step in discovering your values is to look at the list of values you have so far and consider, if a head hunter contacted you and offered you a new job, what would they have to offer you on top of those in order for you to say "hang on a minute, let me close the door, tell me more!". Add those new words to your list by writing them down now. Is there anything else that would tempt you out of your current job if you had all of those other things on your list? If so, add it to your list. Give yourself time here to really go deep and explore all possibilities and notice what comes up. It's easy to discount, but we want you to acknowledge what you need. This is important.

Looking at your list again, ask yourself if you had all of this in your career, is there anything else that would encourage you to stay? You are taking a look through the other lens here. Let's bring this to life in a different way. Let's say you are in a senior HR position right now and you are thinking of leaving because your values of growth and freedom aren't being fulfilled and you resign. What would your boss have to offer you for you to change your mind and choose to stay? Add any new words that come up to your list.

Now take ten minutes to rank the values according to their value to you. Your number one value is the one that is most important to you. You wouldn't sacrifice it for any of the other words on your page.

When you have this one, what's the next most important thing on the list for you in your career? Follow that process until you have your values in a list. You may find as you do this that there are a few values that you think are actually part of the same thing. You may choose to consolidate these into one word or pick one of the words to keep and delete the others as for you, that word encapsulates them all. For example, you may have recognition, reward and praise. You may decide they are all part of recognition for you and feel a stronger connection to that word, so delete reward and praise from your list if they don't stand out as different for you. Or you may identify a new word that encapsulates them all, for example, connection or existence.

Now you will have your values in a list from most important to least important. If you haven't already then, we suggest you write it out as a clean list.

The final step is to test this order. Split your list of words into two – so, if you have ten values, write a list of the top five in one column and then values six to ten in another. Ask yourself honestly, which would you choose? If the order is correct, you will pick the first easily and effortlessly. If not, re-work until the order feels aligned.

Now you have your career values list – congratulations! This is significant as it is your compass for your career decisions. Next, you're going to bring the meaning of these to life, so you can really understand what your values mean to you. This activity will deepen your self awareness and increase the choices you have. You're going to create a values charter by reflecting on examples of how you get your values met.

For example:

My value of learning is met when:

- I read something I've never read before
- When I sign up to a new course
- When someone says something that sparks a new perspective in me
- When something shifts inside me and I get excited about growing

Here's another example. My value of belonging is met when:

- I can pick up where I left off with a friend, even if we haven't spoken in months
- I feel safe with people
- I am included with a smile and genuine warmth
- I am talked about fondly when I am not present

Your turn. Take each of your values and compete the following sentence, then come up with at least four bullet points of what's happening that enables that value to be fulfilled. Just like in the examples above.

My value of _____ is met when _____.

For each of the sentences you created, follow it with your answers to the questions below to deepen your understanding of what your values mean for you and how it informs your decision making. This will exponentially grow your confidence in understanding and articulating your needs.

What needs to be in place for that to happen?

How in control of that are you?

What could you do to be more in control of that?

Knowing your values is important when you make career decisions because the two need to be aligned. When they are, you'll be confident that your decision will bring you your greatest joy in your career. Perhaps, in the past, you have made decisions based on other people's expectations of what you 'should' achieve in your career? For example, influential figures in your life, or perhaps what your organisation views as your career trajectory. Now is the time to reconnect to who you are and what decisions will honour your values.

Now you know your career values and have an order from most important to least important, you can use them to establish the gap from where you are now career wise, to where you want to be. Is there a value that is not being fully met currently?

Draw a table with four columns. In the first column write out your top ten values.

Now, think about the time in your career that was most fulfilling and in the second column, score your values out of ten based on that time.

In the third column, give each value a score from ten based on how fulfilled you feel against it in your current role.

The final column is for you to note down what score you would like each value to be in twelve months time. This isn't necessarily about making everything a ten. Think carefully about how you'd like to be experiencing your work twelve months from now.

What are the gaps? What has this activity bought to the surface for you. Take a few moments to capture your reflections.

What needs to change so that you can achieve those twelve month scores? Capture what actions you can take in the short and medium term that will help you to nudge your values scores in the right direction.

We hope by now you are beginning to see how knowing your values can bring clarity around what you need from your career. When you honour your values and set boundaries around your needs, you excel with purpose. To bring this to life, we'll share a little bit about our stories. How much of it you can relate to?

Jo's story

It was during my coaching training that I discovered my values of warmth, safety, adventure, achievement, learning, growth and flexibility. I have used these values as lighthouses for my career decision making and whilst I was still training in coaching, I decided to leave my current role and set up in business as a coach. The pivotal moment for me was comparing how I was honouring my values in my current role to what I wanted it to be and I realised that leaving would enable me to fulfil more of my values. It gave me the confidence to resign and whilst it was a big decision, it intuitively felt right.

Once I knew my career values, the next steps became obvious. I am so thankful I was introduced to them. They had always been there in the background, but bringing them into focus changed everything. It was the clarity and confidence I needed to make a change. If it wasn't for identifying my values, I may not be here writing this book for you now. I have become a global award-winning coach as a result of behaving in alignment with my strengths and values.

Zoe's story

My values include freedom, learning, achievement, connection and existence. I discovered these values when I worked with my own coach and they were the final piece of the puzzle I needed to be confident that my future career was outside of the corporate world.

I'd always known that I wanted my own business, but I never fully embraced that desire. I had a brilliant role, in a great organisation, with a supportive boss and wonderful team! On paper, I had it all, but I knew there were some missing pieces. I felt I could have more impact. I craved more freedom and I had an insatiable appetite for achievement. No matter what projects I took on, I never felt fully satisfied.

When I looked at my values and did the activities we shared with you here, I realised that I could never fully experience the freedom I wanted whilst working for someone else, and my achievement driver couldn't be fully satisfied because I didn't have the full freedom to choose where to take risks.

Discovering my value of existence was a breakthrough moment for me. This value, for me, encompasses making a difference, leaving a legacy and having an impact in the world. It's about feeling, deep in my core, that I am making a meaningful contribution, and whilst the company I worked for had strong ethics, I was too far from the impact I wanted to have in the world.

My values didn't tell me to train as a coach, but when I looked at what was possible in a career as a coach, I could see I'd be able to tick off every single one of my values. It was a fit and it was all I needed to take my next step, so I self-funded my coaching training and started working towards my own business. It was the first time I'd invested in my own development and it felt amazing. Fast forward the clock to today and that single decision has enabled me to impact thousands of lives and enjoy achievements like a number one podcast.

So that's values - a compass in life and a roadmap for your career. Living life in alignment with your values is guaranteed to bring you more joy and inner peace. Values are one of the main pillars of coaching. Beliefs are another and so we turn our attention to those in the next chapter.

REFLECTION QUESTIONS

As we draw this chapter to a close, let's finish with some questions for you to reflect on to help you connect with your career values and how they can help you to make a confident decision about coaching:

What have you learned about your values?

How does knowing your values give you more clarity about your career direction?

What might this mean for you and your goals?

CHAPTER SUMMARY

The key learning points from this chapter include:

1. Values are unconscious drivers that influence your decision making, your emotional responses and your motivation.
2. Knowing your values creates a compass for life and makes decision making easier, creating confidence and clarity.
3. Living life in line with your values brings more joy, fulfilment and ease.

BELIEFS

> *"Beliefs are not facts. We have the power to change our limiting beliefs into empowering ones so we can create the life we want to live"*
>
> — *JO WHEATLEY & ZOE HAWKINS*

B eliefs are decisions that we made in the past. We often don't think of them as decisions because we perceive them as facts. However, these decisions from the past can hold us back from making the right decision for us in the present, for the future! The key to being able to make great decisions is being able to understand how our beliefs influence the decision and the consequences. It's about identifying our limiting beliefs and changing them to empowering ones so we can move forward positively, satisfying our values.

Beliefs are another core pillar of coaching and influence your decision making in a profound way. We're going to delve into what beliefs are, why they're important, how they influence your behaviour and what you can do to align your beliefs to what you want. Doing this work can enable you to resolve inner conflict holding you back from fully embracing your goals and needs.

Feeling conflicted is normal when you're making an important decision. As human beings, we value predictability as it helps us to feel safe. Inner conflict exists when we have a part of us that believes one thing and another part that believes another. For example, a part of you may believe that you'd be successful training as a coach and launching a coaching business and another part of you may believe you aren't unique enough to make that a success.

Inner conflict also occurs where we believe our values are in conflict. For example, you may value the freedom that a career as a coach offers, but also value the security that your corporate role provides and you may currently believe that it's not possible to fulfil both needs in a role as a coach.

We talked about values in the last chapter. Values and beliefs are connected. Each value you have has a number of beliefs attached to it, some positive and some negative. To fulfil your values, your beliefs need to support them. As you work through this chapter, we'll be helping you to identify the beliefs you hold about your career and the changes you want to make. This is important because we hold beliefs as facts, meaning they can empower us or limit us. When it comes to making important decisions that honour your values, you need to ensure that there aren't any old, outdated beliefs sabotaging you.

Let's explore further what we mean by beliefs. Beliefs are essentially rules we live our life by. They are decisions we made at a point in time that we hold to be true. They were often created to keep us safe. We form beliefs about ourselves and the world around us and these beliefs determine how we experience the world.

Our beliefs are formed from our early childhood experiences, when we are making sense of who we are and how we need to be in the world. If you think about what your experiences were during your early years, you will begin to connect with beliefs that you were taught and that you inferred from hearing conversations and watching behaviour. Beliefs can be 'handed down to us' through generations, or formed ourselves from the significant emotional experiences we have in our early years.

Pause for a moment and write down a belief about your career that was formed during that time frame. A belief Jo grew up with was you can achieve anything you put your mind to, and Zoe believed that when you put the effort in, you get the results you want.

Let's delve a little deeper. Beliefs can be empowering or disempowering. We call positive, enabling beliefs, empowering beliefs and beliefs that hold us back, disempowering or limiting beliefs. For example, I may hold the empowering belief that I can do anything I put my mind to. I may have formed this belief because I had caregivers that showed me love and encouragement, helped me to challenge myself and let me fail, and supported me to try again and again. Here are some other examples of empowering beliefs related to career:

- I am capable
- I am equal
- I am a fast learner
- I am resourceful
- I am resilient
- I will progress
- I am valuable

Take a few minutes to write five empowering beliefs that you hold about deciding to pursue a career in coaching.

Here are some other examples of limiting beliefs we hear from clients related to career:

- I am not a leader
- I am not valuable
- I am not good at change
- I am not good enough
- I am not ready
- I am not likeable
- I am not important

Note down five limiting beliefs that you have about deciding to pursue a career in coaching.

How beliefs are formed is less important than what we can do with them once we know they're there, as we act as if our beliefs are true. They are windows through which we see the world and influence our behaviour. For example, imagine two people at the same career crossroads. Both are considering pursuing a career in coaching. Both long for more impact and an ability to make a real difference through their roles, yet they hold different beliefs. Person one believes that they can successfully become a world class coach, working with leaders all around the world, whereas person two believes that there is too much risk because there are already too many coaches in the market and they will never stand out enough to get clients and earn a living.

How do you think these two people are finding their decision making experience? What do you think will happen?

It's likely that person one is feeling pretty confident about their decision and is already building their plan to make it happen, whereas person two is wracked with self-doubt. It's likely they'll stay lingering on the decision for months, even years and not take any action that moves them closer to what they want.

Notice the emotions that accompany the beliefs. Person one has beliefs that support their decision to build a fulfilling career, and so they feel confident. In taking action, they're likely to feel positive, excited and motivated by their decision. It's a virtuous circle. Person two is experiencing self-doubt; they're likely to feel confused, maybe overwhelmed. They are likely to feel frustrated because they know what they want, they just don't feel like they can achieve it. It's a vicious circle.

Person two, who held the belief that there are already too many coaches in the world, didn't create that belief without good reason; they formed the belief out of a need for protection. This is the positive intent. The key to changing limiting beliefs into empowering beliefs is understanding that all beliefs have a positive intent. This means that they were created for a positive reason. Positive intent is often to do with safety and protection. To find out what the positive intent of a limiting belief is, you can ask yourself - what does the limiting belief get for me, that is positive, despite the fact that it limits me in a number of ways? Then you can ask yourself questions such as "How can I feel safe to achieve my goal?" or, "How is my life different now to when my belief was created?". Below are three examples of limiting beliefs, the positive intent behind them and a potential alternative empowering belief that could help with decision making:

Example one:

Limiting Belief: I'll never make the same amount of money as I do in my employed role working as a coach

Positive Intent: Maintaining financial security

Alternative Empowering Belief: Other people have successful careers as coaches so I can too

Example two:

Limiting Belief: I've never run a business before so I won't be successful as a coach

Positive Intent: Safety from failing

Alternative Empowering Belief: There is no such thing as failure, only lessons and I am an able learner

Example three:

Limiting Belief: People won't see me as credible if I leave my employed role

Positive Intent: Protection from judgement

Alternative Empowering Belief: People will find it inspiring that I took such courageous action, or, what I feel about my career is the only thing that matters

The compound effect of our beliefs is significant as our beliefs influence the thoughts we have, the emotions we feel and the actions we take (our behaviour). The good news is that beliefs can change. They change naturally over time. They also change as the result of significant emotional events. Coaches can help clients to break unhelpful cycles of thoughts, feelings and behaviours by identifying, challenging and supporting clients to change their beliefs in order to achieve the goals that they want. It's one of the best ways to achieve our goals and aspirations.

The reason coaches are necessary when it comes to beliefs is because beliefs reside in your unconscious mind, which means you are not consciously aware of them. Through coaching, you become aware that one of the reasons you may be experiencing internal conflict is because you have beliefs that are not serving you. The problem is you can't change what you can't see and the first step in being able to change your beliefs is identifying them and then understanding how they are holding you back.

Beliefs tend to be in one of three categories; possibility, ability, and worth. Possibility beliefs are about the extent to which you believe something is or isn't possible. Ability beliefs are about your ability to do or be something. Worth beliefs are beliefs you hold about yourself and to what extent you are worthy of receiving what you want. Now we invite you to focus on identifying the beliefs you have about your career decision under each of these three categories. We'll start with the empowering ones. To help you here are a number of empowering beliefs that people deciding to coach often share:

Possibility:

I've made career transitions before so it's possible for me to do it again

I love learning and will enjoy training to be a coach

A career in coaching suits my desire for helping others and having a bigger impact in the world

It is possible to achieve freedom through coaching

Ability:

I have many complimentary skills to bring to a career in coaching

I do a lot of informal coaching already because people often come to me for help and support

I'm a good learner and can learn how to be a great coach

I can build trusting relationships quickly

Worth:

I deserve to be happy in my career

I've worked hard my whole career and can bring so much to the role of a coach

I'm a good person and know I can make a difference to other

I am valuable and have a lot to offer as a coach

Do you share any of these? What others do you hold? Take your time to capture some positive, empowering beliefs that you hold about your career decision under each of the three categories: possibility, ability and worth. What led you to hold these beliefs? This may be feedback from colleagues, a promotion, being in relationship with someone or being invited to contribute to things. Be as specific as you can.

The next step is identifying some of the beliefs that are holding you back from making a confident decision about training to be a coach and setting up a coaching business. Here are some limiting beliefs that we hear from people who are in the process of deciding to train as a coach:

Possibility

The market is saturated with coaches already, there's no room for me

I'll never make enough money as a coach

I'm too busy to do the coaching training

I'm not ready to become a coach yet – it's not the right time

Ability

I don't have the skills to be a great coach

I don't know how to run a successful coaching business

I can't leave the security of my employed role

I could never market or sell myself as a coach

Worth

I'm not good enough to become a coach

No-one would ever buy my services

Everyone else will be better or more experienced than me

People will think it's a ludicrous idea and laugh at me

Make a note of any of the ones you see any of these in yourself and if there are any others that come to mind. As you look at your list of limiting beliefs, select the belief that is holding you back the most and answer the following questions:

What impact is holding this belief having on your life on a day-to-day basis? List at least three things.

How will holding it in the long term (think ten years) restrict and limit your life? The metaphor of carrying a rucksack with your limiting beliefs as heavy stones may resonate with you right now. Do you want to empty the stones out of your bag so you can move forward lightly?

How would your life be different if you didn't believe this and you gave it back to where it belongs?

Now, take a moment to consider the positive intent of this belief. What is the reason you may be holding this limiting belief? What does it do for you that is positive, despite the fact it holds you back in many ways? (Think protection, safety etc.).

Now write out two alternative, empowering beliefs that you would rather have. How does that feel? Complete the sentences below to identify the thoughts and feelings each prompts and the action you'd take if you held those beliefs to be true:

Alternative Empowering Belief one:

If I believed this then I would think.........

If I was thinking that then I would feel.........

If I was thinking and feeling that then I would......(do what?)

Alternative Empowering Belief two:

If I believed this then I would think.........

If I was thinking that then I would feel.........

If I was thinking and feeling that then I would......(do what?)

What evidence do you already have for these beliefs being true? Allow yourself to believe them as if you always held them. Look for and note down three pieces of evidence. The evidence will be there.

What will you choose to do differently with your empowering beliefs in place? Know that you are safe to make choices that empower you. From here on, each day, remind yourself that you have chosen to believe in what serves you and supports the decisions you want to make.

REFLECTION QUESTIONS

As we draw this chapter to a close, let's finish with some questions for you to reflect on to help you define how your belief system is helping or hindering you to achieving a values aligned decision:

What have you learned here?

What limiting beliefs have you let go of?

How are your values and beliefs aligned?

CHAPTER SUMMARY

The key learning points from this chapter include:

1. We have empowering beliefs and limiting beliefs.

Identifying our beliefs is the first step to understanding how our goals are affected by our beliefs.

2. Beliefs and values are intrinsically linked. To be able to fulfil your values you need beliefs that support them.

3. Beliefs influence our decision making and our behaviour because we perceive beliefs as facts and act as if they are true.

4. Beliefs change naturally over time and we can choose to change the beliefs that don't serve us.

EMOTIONS

"Emotions have important information for us. They often act as signals for change and carry important learnings for us to notice and act on to live our lives in alignment with our purpose and values"

— *JO WHEATLEY & ZOE HAWKINS*

Making important decisions will inevitably trigger a range of emotions. The emotions you experience will depend upon your values and beliefs and will in turn influence your thoughts and actions, so understanding and learning how to work with our emotions is central to making confident decisions and enjoying a fulfilling career. In this chapter we help you to explore your relationship with your emotions and get clarity on how your thoughts and feelings are connected to your decision making.

Emotions are our universal human experience. We experience a number of emotions on a daily basis. Emotions are energy, passing through us. An emotion's natural preference, as energy, is to keep on moving, but sometimes they get trapped. It can be helpful to think of them metaphorically as a river of emotions running in front of you everyday. Sometimes an emotion can get stuck, metaphorically, in the river bank. There are times it can dislodge itself in ten minutes, other times it takes a storm or someone else helping to release it. When you think about how you feel about your career right now, are you stuck in an emotion?

Emotions have important information for us. They often act as signals for change and carry important lessons for us to notice and act on, so we can live more in alignment with our purpose and values. Everyone has a different relationship with their emotions. Some people experience fear of being flooded by their emotions, where emotions are felt so strongly that they can be overwhelming. It can feel like they are going to swallow you up, as if the emotions are bigger than you. When this happens, it can make it hard to communicate your needs because you're feeling everything with such force that you can't make sense of them. You may feel small in comparison to the weight and size of your emotions.

Other people can experience what we call emotional stonewalling. This is where emotions are metaphorically packed away into a compartment within you and ignored. People who experience emotional stonewalling often perceive showing emotion as a sign of weakness and so they choose not to acknowledge emotions. They hide them from themselves and others. The challenge with this is that unresolved or unacknowledged emotions build up over time and it can make it difficult to talk about emotions when you need to because your fear is that if you let one out, you may never regain control over them. Unfortunately, what often happens is that the emotions burst out after a period of time and when you least expect or want them to.

The good news is we are able to change our relationship with our emotions if we choose to. For those of you who experience flooding, you can learn to identify and process each emotion in turn and if you're aware you tend to stonewall your emotions then you can learn to build your emotional tolerance. Emotional tolerance is our capacity and ability to invite in, feel and communicate our emotions. Emotions are at the root of our behaviour so it's important for us to develop our emotional literacy and confidence in order to identify and release a stuck emotion, such as fear, which may keep us trapped in indecision.

What we've found from our own experience and in thousands of hours of coaching is that many people find it difficult to identify and name their emotions. Being able to identify your emotions is the first step to building confidence with them. Understanding your emotions helps you to fully connect with your needs and once you understand your needs, you can seek ways to get them met. Ultimately, this enables you to become unblocked and return to a state of flow, able to take action and make decisions that are attuned to your values. So, in this chapter we're going to help you to connect to the emotions you feel about deciding to coach and how they're influencing your decision making.

To help with this, it's useful to understand the six principles to emotional freedom.

1. Emotions Are Neither Good Nor Bad

People often label emotions as good or bad, yet the reality is that it's only our thinking that makes them so. For example, if you think that anxiety is a bad emotion, when you experience it, you want to get rid of it, as quickly as you can, because you perceive it to be bad and this makes you uncomfortable or afraid. Instead, if you accept that emotions are information, when you experience anxiety, you can enquire "What is this anxiety for?", "What is this emotion here to help me with?" or "What does this anxiety need to be able to pass through?". That can then lead you to enable the emotion to get unstuck and continue taking the actions that help you move towards achieving our goal.

Relating to your emotions in this way removes the automatic behaviours that you may have associated with particular emotions and gives you space to reflect, learn and grow.

2. You Are Not Your Emotions

Do you find yourself saying things like "I am frustrated"? The reality is that you are not frustration itself. You are feeling frustrated. When you say things like "I am frustrated" or "I am scared" you limit yourself from being able to process the emotion. Notice how, when you express it as "I am feeling scared or I am feeling frustrated", a healthy distance is created between you and your emotions and in that space, you have the capacity for choice. It depersonalises it, and this is a strategy that can help you to stop feeling flooded by your emotions and create space so that you can process them and develop a healthier relationship to them.

Removing the over identification with an emotion enables you to take the learning that is needed and move forward positively, continuing to experience the full spectrum of emotions available to you in a way that is healthy for you.

3. Emotions Are Unmet Needs

Emotions are linked to your values. When you live life in alignment with your values and take actions to honour them, you feel at peace, fulfilled. However, when you are misaligned, you can feel frustrated, bored, or unsettled. Emotions are information about your needs and signs that something is not being met, for example when you experience emptiness one possible need which is unmet is stimulation. When you feel isolated, a possible unmet need is connection and love, or with overwhelm the unmet need might be about simplification.

Bringing it back to you, if you are feeling confused what is your unmet need? Perhaps it is knowledge - knowledge of what the steps are to becoming a successful coach. Once you meet that need the confusion will float away.

4. Emotions Are Not Always Authentic

Within the field of transactional analysis (a coaching psychology and theory about child development and communication) there is a concept called 'racket feelings'. This means that sometimes you may feel you're experiencing one feeling, whereas in reality it's masking your authentic feeling. For example, you think you are feeling anger, when in fact, it is sadness that you feel. How does this happen? Think about if during childhood you were not allowed to show anger. You still experienced this anger and all the energy associated with it and needed to express and release it in some way. Over time you learned that it was acceptable to show sadness and so as an adult, when you feel angry, you may find yourself crying. You, and certainly others, may interpret this as sadness. The problem is the unmet need of anger is not fulfilled as people respond to sadness. When you feel angry you may not want a hug. Understanding what emotional rackets you have and when they show up can be really helpful to you understanding your feelings about leaving your current role and becoming a coach.

Let's check in for a moment. Do you experience sadness and feel tearful when you think about your work? Could you be angry with your current employer for your role not fulfilling you? Are there any emotions that you think you're feeling that may have a different authentic feeling underneath? What does that mean for you and your career decision making?

5. Emotions Are Linked To Our Thoughts And Our Actions.

Our emotions are intrinsically linked to our thoughts and our actions. Some people are led by their emotions first, others are led by their thoughts and some people simply take action and think and feel after.

It is helpful to be able to understand how they are linked. For example, if I feel optimistic about coaching as a career for me, this may trigger a thought of "it's time to change". Putting the optimism and the thought that it's time to change together may result in the action of signing up to train as a coach and set up a coaching business.

Understanding that our emotions, thoughts and actions are connected gives us choice. If the combination of our current thoughts, feelings and actions are not serving us then we can experiment with changing one of them and exploring the impact it has on the others and if it results in serving our goals and values better. For example, if I have a feeling of apathy about my career, which triggers a thought of "what's the point" and then results in the action of doing nothing, I could experiment with changing my thinking to "I have the ability to get motivated to change", which may trigger an emotion of excitement and combined, may lead to an action of undertaking research. It's a domino effect.

How are your thoughts, feelings and behaviours linked? Are they serving you in a positive way? What do you want to think, feel and do about your career next steps?

6. You Can Choose Your Emotions

When we are coaching and also training coaches, we often hear people say "when they did X it made me feel........". This is a disempowering statement as it suggests that someone else can control your emotions.

What if you believed you could choose your emotional response? You may or may not agree with a person's actions, but we have the ability to choose how we respond and the emotions that these responses generate.

So those are the six principles of emotional freedom:

1. Emotions are neither good nor bad.
2. You are not your emotions
3. Emotions are unmet needs
4. Emotions are not always authentic
5. Emotions are linked to our thoughts and our actions
6. You can choose your emotions

Which of these principles will help you the most in your decision to become a coach?

A challenge many people face is being able to identify their emotions in the first place. There are hundreds of emotions and yet most people can probably only name about seven. There are so many emotions and lots of people get stuck experiencing life within a limited range of emotions. The more you can extend your emotional range the more enjoyable life becomes and the more you are able to understand your needs and get your needs met. The more you can move forward positively, achieving your goals. As someone who is interested in training as a coach it is important you do self work to enable you to widen your emotional vocabulary and emotional awareness. Here is a way for you to do that. Below you can see an example of an emotions wheel. The emotions wheel is a tool widely available and developed originally from the work of Robert Plutchik.

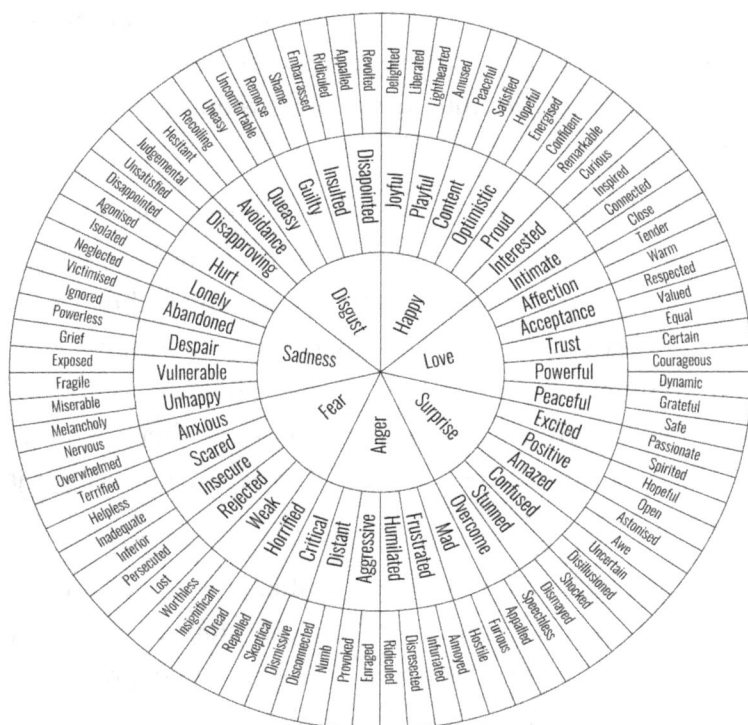

You'll see that the emotions wheel has three rows of emotions. Starting with the inner circle of emotions and then expanding out to the middle row of related emotions and finally the outer ring.

Thinking about your situation right now, deciding to coach, which emotion in the inner ring best represents the emotion you're feeling?

You'll see that the emotion you have chosen fans out into further types of your primary emotion. Which of those is most accurate for you? Great, now take a look at the outer ring, which of those two types of the second ring emotion is the authentic emotion you experience? What does that emotion signal to you as your unmet need? What action can you take to get that need met?

In our experience, high achievers often sacrifice their emotional wellbeing for their need to achieve and drive forward. You are capable of high achievement, but the real goal is achieving in an area where you also benefit from feeling the emotions you want to feel. How aligned is your current role and future prospects, if you stay where you are, to your emotional wellbeing? Is it time for change to bring them both together?

You can take this emotions work further by considering your relationship to your emotions. You can start by identifying what emotions were welcomed in your home growing up and which ones were not. What did you do with those emotions?

You may notice patterns in your relationship with your emotions. Are you confident with your emotions or is there a fragility there that is holding you back? What would you discover if you did an emotional audit?

Questions like this provide the types of exploration you will learn to do with your clients when you train to be a coach. You may look at some of these questions and think "I've never asked myself that before!". Now is a great time – be curious. We recommend self work as part of your actions before and during training as a coach.

Let's dive deeper into understanding the emotions you feel about your career currently. Complete these sentences:

I feel _____in my career

Write out as many of these statements as come to mind. Here are some examples:

I feel bored in my career

I feel frustrated in my career

I feel stuck in my career

Next, add on a connecting 'thought statement" about the thought that is triggered by the emotion.

Here are some examples:

I feel bored in my career and I think I need a change

I feel stuck in my career so I think I am failing

We're going to look at how those thoughts and feelings influence your behaviour. Knowing that you have those feelings, and those thoughts, how is that influencing your behaviour?

In our example this may look like:

I feel bored in my career and I think I need a change so I am researching different career choices I could make;

or

I feel stuck in my career, I think I am failing and so I'm panicking about what to do next and not trusting any of my decisions.

Not everyone starts with feelings. Some start or lead with thoughts, in which case your paragraph may start with "I'm thinking I need a career change, so I'm feeling curious and I'm researching how I might create a career as a coach".

You might be reading this book, feeling a bit unsure about what to do with your career next. Your sentences above may read something like "I am feeling confused about what's best for my career and I am thinking I don't know how to make a decision and so I am stagnating". If this is the case, you can use the same process to help you access more productive thinking and feeling. It starts by asking yourself, what is a positive thought that could be more helpful? Perhaps I think I am good at knowing what brings me joy, or I am good at problem solving. Write out a more positive thought.

Next, step into that positive thought and notice what feelings that generates for you. Perhaps it's about feeling more in control, or calmer.

Lastly, what impact does having that thought and those feelings have on your behaviour. Perhaps it is being more focused or proactive? What's the impact on your behaviour now?

Let's pause here. What has this activity shown you about your emotions so far? What have you learned about how they are connected to your thoughts and behaviours? What's emerging for you as action you want to take?

There are some particular emotions that can peak when we consider change. One of those is grief. The reason for this is that change inherently involves loss. It can involve loss of many kinds. In The Coaching Crowd podcast, Zoe and Jo talk about their transition from HR to coaching and the loss of their HR identity. Other losses that can be experienced when we change career:

- Loss of predictability
- Loss of close friendships
- Loss of the life you thought you were going to lead a few years ago
- Loss of the regular commute
- Loss of status
- Loss of financial security

When we change our regular routine, that feels safe and familiar, it can feel destabilising, until a new one becomes established. It is important that losses are acknowledged. With all change there is a letting go as well as a welcoming in that is required to transition well. Here are some questions to help you acknowledge and begin to process a change, enabling you to let go and welcome in, in a healthy way:

- What needs to be honoured here?
- What needs to be forgiven?
- What do I need to accept gracefully?
- What am I saying yes to?
- What am I saying no to?
- What learning is available to me here that will enable me to let go easily and effortlessly?

REFLECTION QUESTIONS

As we draw this chapter to a close, let's finish with some questions for you to reflect on to help you define how your emotions can help you to make the right decision for you:

What have you learned about your emotions that is helpful for your decision making?

How are you now feeling about your career decisions?

What might that feeling be telling you?

CHAPTER SUMMARY

The key learning points from this chapter include:

1. Emotions are energy, they want to keep flowing, but sometimes they get stuck.

2. The relationship you have with your emotions affects your thoughts and actions.
3. You can learn a lot from identifying your emotions and taking time to appreciate what we need to learn.
4. You can empower yourself with your emotions by learning to choose your emotional response.
5. Extending your emotional range will enable you to get your needs met.

IDENTITY

"People can struggle to make the leap when their career has become synonymous with who they are. You are so much more than your job title".

— *JO WHEATLEY & ZOE HAWKINS*

Who you think you are directly impacts the decisions you make. Career transition is more than changing what you do, it goes to the core of who you are. As you face into deciding what to do with your career, unconsciously you'll be questioning what that will mean for you and whether the change fits the image of who you believe you are deep down. Your identity helps you to decide where you think you'll belong, how you'll be perceived and where you'll feel safe. If your identity feels threatened, it can be difficult to make the changes that you want to make.

The challenge is you have many identities and your identities naturally want to evolve. This can create confusion when making important decisions and lead to internal conflict. In your personal life, you may have an identity as a mother or father, a sister or brother, a spouse, a friend or a neighbour, for example. When it comes to work, you may have an identity as a professional, high potential, coach, entrepreneur, CEO or a business partner. Your identities influence what you believe is or isn't possible for you. As coaches, we've supported many people to make decisions about their own career transition. What we notice is that people struggle to make the leap when their career has become synonymous with who they are.

Sometimes, your values and your work can become so intrinsically linked that you can't separate yourself from your work. It's not just your values that influence this; your beliefs do too. For many people, their sense of self worth and value is wrapped up in achievements and work, believing that they are only worthy if they are working hard or earning money etc. The truth is you are worthy whether or not you are doing these things. Everyone is born worthy. It's your experiences that lead you to question this. Therefore, when it comes to pivoting in your career, you may be buffering against a level of inner conflict around your identity.

Have you ever been in a situation where you have found yourself saying "I'm not that sort of person", "that's just not me" or "that's just who I am?". These are your identities at play. When you experience something that doesn't fit with how you see yourself, it can feel jarring and create an inner tension.

Identities are important when it comes to goals and decision making because when you want to achieve something, it needs to be aligned to how you see yourself, otherwise, you won't be able to achieve your goal in the way you want to. You'll get stopped in your path when you become misaligned. In order to achieve something, we need to be able to be, or become, the version of ourselves that is achieving that goal. Then align our values, beliefs, skills and behaviours to this version.

This leads us into the challenge of "who am I if I'm not [insert profession]". Take us as examples. We were Fellow HR professionals with the Chartered Institute of Personnel & Development (UK Body for HR Professionals). We were short listed for an award with them and had been paid members our whole career. We had worked our way up through the levels and this had been one of our benchmarks of professional achievement. We were successful in our HR careers and if anyone asked what we did we'd say, "I work in HR" or I'm an "HR Director" (Jo) or "I'm a Global Organisational Development Consultant" (Zoe). It always included HR. There was safety and credibility involved in being at the top of our profession and belonging to something. A sense of achievement and that fitted with our identity.

It can be challenging to think about going from a senior position in one profession to starting afresh in a new one. You fear feeling deskilled. The reality is that all the experience and knowledge you have gained previously is valuable and you take it with you. It will compliment your next step. It can enable you to gain credibility in your new profession even quicker. You'll unlearn some things and also learn new things. You are so much more than your job title. Transitioning careers is really about extending your career rather than changing it in its entirety.

Shifting from one identity to another involves letting go and the key here is to notice what needs to be honoured to make the transition natural and healthy. Let's start by unearthing some of your identities related to deciding to coach, in an activity called "my three identities". The three identities we'll look at here are your work identity, your authentic identity and your fear identity and all you need to do is answer the questions honestly and authentically with the first things that come into your mind when you read the questions.

Your **Work Identity** – this is the curated version of yourself that you believe you need to achieve your career goals.

What does your career tell you about who you are?

How does your career contribute to your feelings of worth and value?

How does your career contribute to your confidence?

What has your career taught you about what you do well?

What do you value most about your career?

What do people say about you when you are not in the room at work?

What are you most recognised for in your career?

Your **Authentic Identity** – this is who you are naturally, even when you are really tired or up against it.

Who are you when no one is watching at work?

What positive things do you know about yourself that others may not see?

What parts of yourself are you hiding at work?

How do you most like to spend your time?

Who do you most like to be around?

Now complete these sentences – this is your **Fear Identity**.

My greatest fear about deciding to coach is……

If I am not [insert current role] then I am …………

Without my work, how will I show people that I'm ……………

I need my work to give me …………

Take a moment to consider what this activity has revealed for you. What have you learned?

It is completely normal to have discovered something that's in your way. Here's some of the blocks we commonly see preventing coaches from stepping into a new identity:

- Not having any role models or examples of business owners in their family – "We are not business owners, we are employees"

- Being wedded to only one version of success – "Success is getting a secure job and climbing the career ladder"
- Being attached to their identity as a professional and what this means to them and others – "I am a [insert profession]", other people respect me because of what I do
- Having strong emotions come up at the thought of transitioning out of their employed role. Emotions such as fear, guilt or sadness
- Not wanting to stand out and do something different, needing to be accepted and belong – e.g. "I work in the city, where all my friends and colleagues work too"

There are many others too. What do you see in yourself? Like all mindset hurdles, you can work through any that come up and one way to start to do that is to write a letter to the block that feels most significant to you. This isn't just any letter, it's a letter written from your unconscious mind, to explore and release what is holding you back from fully embracing a new identity. You let your hand do the writing, rather than your head.

The way to write the letter is to write it in the first person, for example "Dear fear" then you can write three paragraphs:

The first paragraph is about your relationship to the blocker in the past.

The second is about your relationship to it in the present.

The third is about your relationship to it in the future.

Once you've written your letter, read it aloud to yourself.

Here is an example letter so you have an idea of what yours may look like. Of course, it may look different too – whatever you write is just perfect.

Dear CEO pathway,

In the past, I was excited by you. I was honoured that I was chosen to walk the CEO pathway. I worked so hard to become recognised and valued at work. I put in long hours, missed time with my family for late meetings, travelled the world to build my network and grow my influence. Part of me was proving that I could do it, I craved the validation that I could be something or someone. To know that I was on that pathway bought me excitement and joy.

Lately though, I've lost the love for it. I've begun to notice that there is so much more to life than work. I feel like I've missed some of the precious years of my children growing up, chasing a dream that I'm not sure I need anymore. I'm still ambitious, I'm still driven, but when I look to the future, it looks a bit empty. I'm not sure I want to be hopping from hotel room to hotel room whilst my family are at home waiting for me. I'm not sure I can honestly stand there and encourage people to follow the same path, because the world of work needs to change. I don't want or need to chase the money anymore; I'm feeling a craving for more meaning and purpose. I'm not 100% sure what that is yet, but I don't think it's you. I want permission to move away from you and forge my own path. One where I can live in alignment with my values.

In the future, I want to enjoy a thriving career without you. I want to feel whole and fulfilled without needing you to prove that I am good enough. I want to believe that I am resourceful and capable of walking my own path and in doing so, find that meaning and purpose I crave, and I want to be present with my family and loved ones. Not always having one foot out the door or one eye on my emails. My version of success isn't going to be someone else's pathway, it's going to be what I need it to be. Myself as CEO of my own business. One that is 100% aligned to my values.

So, thank you for the adventure, thank you for being there when I needed you. Thank you for teaching me so much about life and business, but I don't need you anymore. It's time for us to part, I've got to do this next bit on my own.

Yours,
Sign off with your name

Have a go now and write your letter.

How does that feel? What have you learned?

As coaches, we are continually exploring our own identities. Permission is key when it comes to identity. Do you give yourself permission to change? What would need to happen for you to give yourself permission to be more than one thing? Just as we can choose and change our beliefs, we can also align and upgrade our identity to who we want and need it to be so we can achieve our goals with ease.

Connecting to your future self can be a helpful strategy to shift an out-of-date identity. Your future self is a version of you that has already achieved your goal. They've done the work, overcome the obstacles, taken the learning, applied it and continued moving forward until they have achieved the goal. Working with your future self is a way to show your unconscious mind what to focus on and who to become. Also, what is possible and, in another reality, has already been achieved. Let's begin. Imagine you are the future version of yourself that has made your career pivot, trained as a coach and are now enjoying a rewarding career working in alignment with your values and purpose as a coach. Really step into this. We invite you to write down your answers to the following questions from that place:

What will you be hearing? What will people be saying around you? What will you be seeing? How will you be feeling when you have achieved your goal?

Then, from that place in the future, imagine you are looking back on your current state, and notice all the work you've done, all the effort you've taken, all the milestones you've surpassed to achieve what you have and ask yourself, what have you learned on this journey to achieving your goals? Who are you now that you've achieved these goals?

Take time to think about what's working for you now you've achieved these goals? How does it feel to be the version of yourself that has achieved these goals? From this point in the future, as you celebrate who you have become and all that you have learned, what advice, guidance or wisdom does your future self have for your current self?

You're doing great work here. Read back through your answers. What are you noticing as you read them? What is happening to your identity? Is there room for it to shift? Are you reconnecting with the person you were always meant to be? What is happening to the energy inside you?

The important thing to remember is that who you are and what you do are two separate things, and who you are at various phases of your life will always exist within you. It's about creating space to grow and nurture new versions of yourself and have the courage to let go of the ones that no longer serve you. Remember that those future selves already exist. How can you honour them now in the present so they will be thankful when you meet them in the future?

Perhaps you have outgrown your identity as an employee and your identity as a coach is no longer prepared to take a back seat. That in-between phase is unsettling as you don't feel like you fit into either, and that's ok. That's part of the process of enabling you to fully let go and fully embrace the person you are always meant to be. How exciting would it be for you to be at the forefront of a profession still evolving, where you can contribute and influence its future direction? The coaching profession has so much opportunity for you to be a pioneer.

REFLECTION QUESTIONS

As we draw this chapter to a close, let's finish with some questions for you to reflect on to help you define how your current and future identity are impacting your decision to coach:

What have you learnt about your identity?

How does your identity support your goals?

What do you need to align or upgrade with your identity?

What will you feel and believe when you've done this?

CHAPTER SUMMARY

The key learning points from this chapter include:

1. Our identity needs to be aligned with our goals. If we do not see ourselves as the person who has achieved that goal then we'll remain stuck.
2. We can upgrade and align our identity to our goals once we can see where the disconnect is.
3. Whilst it can feel like you're giving something up

when you're transitioning careers, the reality is that you're extending your career and taking all of your skills and experience with you. No-one is ever really starting from scratch because of all the resources they have gained in their previous experiences.

GOALS

> "Visualising your goal can be transformational. It's a way of focusing our unconscious mind on what we want to achieve"
>
> — ZOE HAWKINS & JO WHEATLEY

Decisions are goals, an action of the mind. They set you on a path to something new. Goals are a way to harness and tap into your passion, they're a source to build strength and talent and enable fulfilment and joy. Knowing how to set them effectively is liberating. It builds positive momentum in your life and career, giving you something to focus your energy on and evaluate your progress against. Ultimately, goals are the manifestation of our thoughts, feelings, values, strengths and beliefs.

The process of setting and achieving a goal gives your unconscious mind evidence of ability and worthiness. The more goals you set and achieve, the more evidence you gather of your ability to learn, grow and be in control of your life, therefore helping you to build confidence and self esteem. These are valuable experiences for life, as well as your career.

What's your relationship to goal setting? Is it something you find enjoyable or is it something you feel lost with? We are going to share insights and information about setting well formed goals with you so that you can get excited and have confidence in knowing you can achieve them.

Goals are another one of the main pillars of coaching. They are a key element that distinguishes coaching from other approaches, as coaching is about having a future focus, taking you from where you are now, to where you want to be. Remember earlier in the book we shared that your conscious mind is your goal setter? You set goals in coaching by evaluating what you want in the future. It's a conscious process, and yet it's your unconscious mind which is your goal getter. Without goals, your unconscious mind will search endlessly for ways to help you to feel fulfilled.

Without goals, your unconscious mind doesn't know what to focus on, yet with clear goals it will notice information which fits with your intentions. So, for example, if you have a goal to train as a coach, as you're scrolling through LinkedIn, you'll notice everyone who is a coach, and all the posts where people have shared they are training to be a coach or looking for clients for their coaching practice hours. Goals are instructions to your unconscious mind on what to pay attention to.

Lots of people don't set goals or they set goals that are unrealistic and get demotivated by them. When goals are too big, you can feel overwhelmed and struggle to take action to get started. When you set goals, you aren't in control of, you can get sidetracked by the fear of failing. You may get stuck because you are afraid. It's normal to be afraid when you are making important decisions. The problem is often created by focusing on the end result rather than the first next step. There is a science to setting goals that help you to feel motivated and energised by your decisions. Breaking goals down helps us to get unstuck and take the actions that matter.

Think about deciding to coach. Your first steps might be picking up the phone and talking to someone who is already a coach and doing some research. It could be to decide you are going to train as a coach and for the next few days, start with the actions of working out the right level of course, your budget etc. It's not about perfection, it's about making progress and learning is always progress. In reality the question is not are you ready, but simply are you ready enough to learn?

Goals are part of everyday life. In work places we have performance reviews which have objectives, there are deadlines for report submissions or targets for sales. We have goals for all areas of our life, fitness, relationships, wealth, health, as well as career. The secret to success is choosing goals that bring you into alignment with your strengths, talents and values, and align your identity and beliefs to what you want to achieve.

So far throughout this book, you've discovered your strengths, and values and created new empowering beliefs to support your decision making. You know how to manage your emotions and upgrade your identity, so it's aligned to what you want. Now, it's time to set a goal and we're going to try on the decision that you do want to become a coach and make a career transition that brings you closer to your purpose.

The first thing to do is decide the eight most important things related to transitioning into a career as a coach. For example, you might have:

1. Research options for coach training
2. Speak to three people who are coaches and find out the reality of working as a coach
3. Review my finances and create a financial plan for transition
4. Build a business plan
5. Read some coaching books
6. Share my decision with friends and family
7. Create a timeline of events that leads up to me becoming a coach
8. Listen to the Coaching Crowd Podcast!

Once you have your eight most important activities, create a wheel with eight segments and in each segment write one of these activities

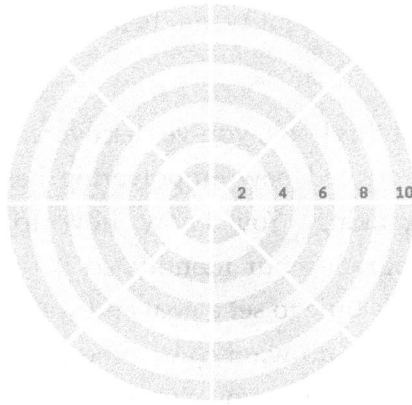

Next, score each area on a scale of 0-10 with 10 being totally complete and 1 meaning you haven't given it any thought at all. After you've scored the areas of the wheel join up the segments together to create a visual representation of where you are at.

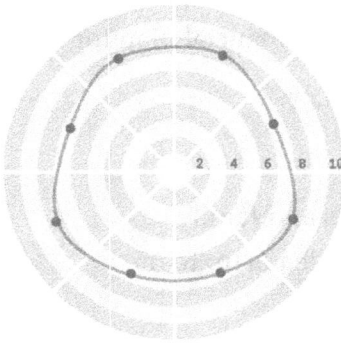

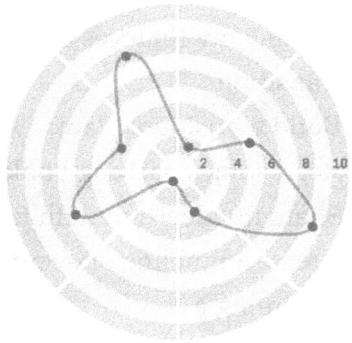

As you complete this activity take a moment to consider these questions.

- What has this exercise revealed for you?
- What else do you notice?
- How is the 'shape' of your wheel impacting on you right now?
- Which areas are below a 6 for you?
- How is this influencing you?
- What would need to happen for you to be able to score this at an 8?
- If you could achieve that, what impact would that have right now?
- What's stopping you from being able to score it at an (8/9/10)?
- What areas are a priority for you?
- What goals are important for you now?

Completing the wheel stimulates thinking and encourages new perspective and insight. In terms of choosing a goal to move forward with, you may choose the area of the wheel which has the lowest score or one where you can make the biggest impact. For the purposes of now, let's choose booking a coaching training qualification.

We're going to share with you a checklist to refine your goal to ensure that you are guaranteed to achieve it and you can enjoy achieving it. It's an activity from the field of NLP and first created by Richard Bandler and John Grinder, who believed it was possible to identify the patterns of thoughts and behaviours of successful individuals and to teach them to others. Write down your answers to each question as you go.

1. What specifically do you want?

Here we want you to state, in the positive, what you want, why you want it and by when you want to have it. If you've written "I don't want" or it's not stated positively, then re-write it until it is a positive statement.

The reason for this is that our unconscious mind cannot process a negative. If you have a goal of 'stop procrastinating" you have to think about procrastinating in order to consider stopping it. Instead, the positive alternative is to think about being more focused, which diverts your attention to what you actually want.

Here's another example, you might be thinking "I don't want to stay in my corporate job forever", that goal puts the focus on staying in that in-house role forever – it doesn't help you. In fact, it hinders you. "I want to book a coaching training qualification by the end of this week" is positive and time lined so it meets the first criteria and you can progress to the next question in the checklist.

2. Do you believe that the goal is achievable?

This means do you believe that it is possible for a human being to achieve this outcome? If it has been done by someone, then in theory, it can be done by you too. If you are the first, find out if it is possible before you proceed to the next step. In our example above, you know that it is possible for you to book a coaching training qualification as many other people, including us, have done it and we are coach trainers so you know through that lens too.

3. What will you accept as evidence that you have your outcome?

Here we are building a sensory picture of when you achieve your goal. What will you see, hear, and feel when you have done what you have set out to do? As you think about and connect with booking a coaching training qualification, what will you be seeing – will it be an email confirming your place on a programme? What will you be hearing – will it be the training providers saying welcome to your coaching qualification, or your friends saying "That's awesome, you'll be amazing at that. You've always wanted to do it"? What will you be feeling when you book your coaching training? Excited, elated, determined, focused, energized, free, proud?

4. Is achieving this outcome within your control? Can you personally do it, authorise it or arrange it?

This is where most goals fall down. When people set goals, they often inadvertently set a goal that they don't have personal control over – for example, earning £100,000 in my first year of business. You are not in control of that £100,000 coming in, you are only in control of the efforts you put in to generate it. If you set goals that you're not in control of it can generate pressure and a fear of failure. Booking a coaching qualification is within your control because it is down to you, so this is well formed. If your goal is being accepted onto a course, you'd need to re-frame that, because it wouldn't be your decision.

5. Are the costs and consequences of achieving your goal acceptable to you?

Is making a decision to book a coaching qualification worth the effort, time and all other investment and impact on third parties? Third parties may be family members, friendships or work colleagues. Identify the consequences that arise and consider if they are worth it in comparison to achieving your goal. If it's a yes then you move to the next question.

6. Do you have or can you obtain all the resources, both tangible and intangible, that you need to achieve your outcome?

Resources can include knowledge, beliefs, environment, people, money, time. There is a lot here, so take each one in turn and note down what you need related to each of these. If you find that you already have everything that you need, progress to the next question. If something is missing, achieving this will become your priority goal and you take that through this questions checklist first as you will need it to achieve the goal you started with.

7. How does achieving your goal honour your values?

When your values are aligned to your goal it ensures that you're wholly motivated to achieve them. If they are not aligned, you'll experience inner conflict and resistance. You identified your career values in the earlier values chapter so how does booking a coaching training qualification honour your career values? If it doesn't, then you need to find a new goal. If it does then fantastic, you move forward to the last question.

8. If you could have it now, would you take it?

This may seem like an obvious yes as you are the one setting the goal. Here though, you need to check a couple of important things. Does this goal really belong to you or is it something that others have placed upon you? When coaching clients, sometimes when they get to this question they say "I have just realised that this goal isn't mine – it's what my parents always wanted for me" and they realise they can put that goal down. Or they realise it's a goal that their manager has placed on them. Other times the answer is "yes, absolutely. That would be amazing!". If it is a yes, definitely, then you have a well formed goal! You will feel like it has momentum and you want to get started now you have alignment.

Setting goals in this way ensures goals are achievable. How are you feeling now about your goal?

Being able to visualise yourself achieving your goals can take this a step further. Visualising your goal can be transformational. It's a way of focusing your unconscious mind on what you want to achieve, giving it a very clear set of instructions. If you can visualize something, you are more likely to be able to achieve it. Can you visualise yourself working as a coach? Imagine getting up each day and helping others to achieve their goals and desires. Where would you be coaching from? What would you wear when you are coaching? As you think of your wardrobe now, is there a particular outfit you can imagine yourself wearing as a coach? Perhaps it's a new look or image that you'll be stepping into. What smells do you associate with this vision of being a coach? Is it drinking coffee in preparation for your coaching sessions or the smell of a candle you'll having burning on your desk as you coach? What sounds do you associate with being a coach? The sound of birds in the garden. The sound of your clients saying "wow, I have never thought of it like this before", or "that's amazing, I feel so happy" or "I'd love to work with you if you'll be my coach?!". The more details you can add to your visualisation of achieving your goal, the more powerful it is for you as a motivator.

You've reached the end of part one and we hope that in working through the chapters and doing the activities, you have reconnected with who you are, have a much deeper understanding of what you need to be fulfilled at work, and how to make that happen. We know you'll have made progress with your decision to coach and that decision is firmly in your hands.

REFLECTION QUESTIONS

As we draw this chapter to a close, let's finish with some questions for you to reflect on to help you define your relationship to goal setting now:

How are you feeling about goal setting and goal achievement now?

What are you motivated to do as your first next steps?

What goals are you in control of?

CHAPTER SUMMARY

The key learning points from this chapter include:

1. Goals are instructions to the unconscious mind so it knows what to focus on.
2. The key to goal setting is setting goals that are aligned to our values and empowering beliefs.
3. When you set goals that you're in control of, it removes fear and ensures we are motivated and excited by our goals.

Part Two

SETTING UP A SUCCESSFUL AND SUSTAINABLE COACHING BUSINESS

"Experience of running a business is not a prerequisite for success. What it takes to have a successful coaching business is a belief in what you are doing, determination, and a willingness and ability to learn ."

- JOANNE WHEATLEY & ZOE HAWKINS

FOUNDATIONS

> *"Knowing how to build a sustainable and successful coaching business enables as many people as possible to benefit from the positive transformations that occur through coaching"*

— *JO WHEATLEY & ZOE HAWKINS*

Welcome to part two of Deciding to Coach. As you dive into part two and start learning all about the business side to coaching, we're going to take a moment to crystallise why you want to coach. When you have a clear "why" for what you are trying to achieve, it gives you laser focused motivation, drive and purpose. It helps you to keep going when you have moments of doubt and uncertainty. Decisions become easier when you know what you are moving towards and why you are doing it, so take some time to connect with your answers to the important questions below:

1. What are your reasons for wanting to leave your employed role?
2. What do you want instead?
3. How does becoming a coach honour your values?
4. What's most important to you about transitioning from your employed role right now?
5. How will your future be different when you make a success of this transition?
6. What's your most compelling "why" for doing this?

You may have lots of reasons, perhaps your 'why' is about your wellbeing and achieving a better balance between your work and your personal life? It may be about making a difference to others, independence or perhaps it's about removing the cap of your earning and feeling free to take risks and drive forward. Whatever your why is, take time to fully connect with it, because it will shape the rest of your decisions about how you build and structure your business.

When we were thinking about training to be coaches, our why was clear, but one of the questions in our mind was how we would eventually leave the corporate world and run a successful business as a coach without any prior experience it. We know we'd have found it helpful to have understood more about the reality of running a coaching business at that stage. Our intention with the second part of this book is to share our experience and what has worked for us so that you can have a head start. We don't want you to get stuck with "how" questions, so we're going to share with you a business model for a successful and sustainable coaching business. Whilst it's not the only business model you can use, it's the one we have seen generate consistent clients and a successful business where we have earned more than in our corporate roles. You'll learn how you can take your coaching business aspirations and make them a reality. We want to set you up for success from the outset. It's also the reason that our coaching courses include access to our Coaching Crowd Business Lounge.

Many of our clients that come on our coaching training programmes focus on gaining their coaching qualification as step one, integrating coaching into their current employed role as step two, before finally going all in and deciding to leave their employed role. Some people that train with us find that integrating coaching into their employed role is enough for them to connect with their purpose and experience more joy. Others find their coaching training accelerates their plan to leave their employed role and set up a coaching business. Whatever deciding to coach looks like for you, know that you get to do it on your terms, in line with your values. What we know from our trainees is that many have questions about what it takes to grow a coaching business or create a side hustle as a way to add more creativity, joy or freedom to the way they work. Whilst this may not be on your plan now, we hope by outlining the aspects involved in business, it enables you to decide if it is something that you'd like to do and give you the confidence to take those steps if it is.

We will always be honest with you. Building a successful business takes time. When you start any business, you need perseverance and tenacity. Setting up a coaching business can challenge your mindset. There will be times when you'll need to dig deep and be courageous as you stride forward. When you have the right mindset and support round you, the rewards personally, professionally and financially are immensely fulfilling. Getting to do what you love everyday and work that around your life will fill you with pride, purpose and satisfaction.

The most important thing to know is that you can absolutely have a successful and sustainable coaching business. Experience of running a business is not a prerequisite for success. What it takes to have a successful coaching business is a belief in what you are doing, determination, and a willingness and ability to learn. In this chapter, we are sharing with you what we see as strong foundations to a coaching business, so you can begin to understand what's involved.

Now that you have your why about setting up a coaching business, let's introduce to you what a successful and sustainable coaching business model looks like and the reality of running a coaching business. There is no one business formula that is guaranteed to bring you results, but there are a number of things that will be helpful for you to consider when starting out, especially if you haven't run a business before or have any experience of sales or marketing.

You may read what's next and feel excited because it all feels so achievable, or you may read it and feel daunted at the sheer idea of some of the activities. Remember, fear is just a response to a perceived threat. Right now, some of these activities might feel nerve-wracking, and that's OK. All new things we learn and commit to can feel daunting at first. What you know now, having read part one, is that you are in control of your mindset and you can choose your response. You have the skills to break any goal down into bite size steps. You will grow in confidence with every step you take. Stay connected to why you're doing this, it's worth the effort.

Let's begin by exploring what we mean by a successful and sustainable coaching business. It's a subjective question because everyone's version of success is different. What we care about is helping you to connect to what this would look like for you because whilst you instinctively may feel you know what it is, as you take time to truly connect with it, you may find that it develops into something different to what you initially envisaged. That vision of success will become more and more compelling and it may speed up your actions to achieve it!

Our definition of a successful and sustainable coaching business is one that provides a predictable and consistent flow of income with confidence about future earning, gained through coaching work that brings joy and fulfilment to us and our clients. It's one where we can:

- Continuously learn
- Be challenged
- Connect with others on a deep level
- Create something that will stand the test of time

- Innovate and be creative
- Feel energised doing what we love, with people we love to work with
- Have autonomy
- Have flexibility around our working hours
- Have financial security for us and our families

The level of income you desire to earn, the number of hours you aspire to work, the way you choose to do that work – that's all for you to define.

For seven years, we ran a business, learning as we went. Having been high achievers from school to the corporate world, we naively assumed we had what it took to build a successful business too and decided we'd learn along the way. Whilst we had success in those years of business, it was unpredictable. Some years were great, others ok, but we didn't have a clear plan for growth or funnel for clients wanting to work with us and we weren't visible enough. We hadn't identified a proven business model.

It definitely would have helped us to have invested time and energy into understanding how to run a business. Honestly though, we didn't know where to get information about how to set up and run a successful coaching business, as those who are successful often keep the secrets to themselves. That's not our approach. We want to ensure that after undertaking world class coaching training, our coaches know step-by-step how to build a sustainable and successful coaching business. This enables as many people as possible to benefit from the positive transformations that occur through coaching.

There are two core pillars of the successful and sustainable coaching business model that have enabled our business to grow significantly:

1. The business is built through community online using attraction marketing
2. The business is built from a portfolio of services

We'll take each of those in turn and talk more about what they are.

1. The Business Is Built Through Community Online Using Attraction Marketing

Social media has become a gateway for a global marketplace, it provides an opportunity for prospective clients to get to know, like and trust you at scale, reaching thousands of people daily. The heartbeat of any great business is customers that trust you and recommend you to others. Your new clients will become your greatest assets in business. Connection is at the heart of coaching. In a coaching relationship, you are creating a safe space for your clients to learn and grow with you. To invest in coaching, a prospective client will need to feel they can trust you. The way to build a successful and sustainable coaching business is to create spaces like this at scale where prospective clients can join you to get to know who you are and how you work. We call these spaces communities. You can create communities in a number of places online, for example:

- Groups on online community platforms
- Email lists

- Instagram followers
- LinkedIn Connections
- Podcast Listeners

Building communities is at the heart of attraction marketing, which is an approach to marketing which sees your clients coming to you, rather than you having to make cold outreach to draw clients in. It's a way for you to give value and become known in the industry for who you are and how you work. This strategy is great for coaches because we know that most coaches are motivated by helping and serving others and that's what this approach is all about.

The core concept of attraction marketing is that you consistently create and share highly valuable content that you know your prospective clients can benefit from. You share this content for free as a way to engage, support and attract prospective clients to your communities. Examples of attraction marketing include:

- A weekly blog
- A weekly top-tips email bulletin
- A regular podcast
- A weekly educational video
- A series of masterclasses

The key is that your content is shared consistently so that your community members know when to expect something from you. As your community members engage with your content, they get to know you, build trust in you and overcome buyer anxiety barriers to working with you in a paid capacity.

Your content needs to be valuable, but not give everything away. It needs to help people with the first few steps of their journey and be enough to lead them to a point where they are ready to work with you. Attraction marketing leads to loyal followers who will recommend you to their friends and peers who they believe would benefit from your content too. It's a significant commitment, but when you find a medium which you enjoy, it can become a fulfilling part of doing business, particularly when you start to receive feedback from your community about how valuable they are finding your work and when they recommend you to others.

2. The Business Is Built From A Portfolio Of Services

Building a portfolio of services is about having a selection of ways of working with you. When you train as a coach, you are taught how to coach in a 1:1 capacity, and it's natural to emerge from a coaching training programme and focus on gaining 1:1 clients. Those clients are an important part of your business, but if you build a business relying solely on 1:1 work, you risk burn out and also limit your ability to scale your business.

The reality of running a business is that you will not be coaching all the time. There is a great deal of work involved in working "on" your business (on creating content for example), as well as the time you'll want to spend working "in" your business (in a client facing capacity).

1:1 coaching is intense work, it takes preparation, concentration and deep listening. In your average working day, assuming your coaching session are 1-1.5 hours long, we wouldn't recommend coaching more than three people. This is a realistic amount of coaching to enable you to protect your energy and show up resourced and fresh for each of your clients. Relying only on 1:1 work therefore limits your growth potential.

Equally, not all prospective clients will be ready to, or want to, engage in 1:1 coaching, so creating a ladder of services where people can join you at different levels of investment will help you to serve more clients who want and need your support and enable you to grow and scale your business.

An example of a ladder of services, with investment increasing as you go, might be:

1. Your free content
2. A low paid masterclass
3. A monthly membership
4. A group coaching programme or course
5. 1:1 coaching

You spread your risk across a portfolio of services so you do not become reliant on any one service you're offering. It can give you protection when markets change. Notice how your business can benefit from being multifaceted. You will also find many clients who work with you at every stage as they grow with you.

At this point you might be thinking "that all sounds like far too much effort, I am not ready for that'. That's ok. Building a business is about doing it on your terms and finding joy in every step. All businesses are built through incremental small steps. It's the compound interest of each of these steps that really makes the difference.

When you're ready for change, you start with step one and keep going. Consistency is key and it's truly what makes the difference. All you need to do at the end of this book is decide your first next step, which, if coaching is for you, is to book onto a coaching training programme and then keep taking steps forward on the business development front.

REFLECTION QUESTIONS

As we draw this chapter to a close, let's finish with some questions for you to reflect on to help you define your version of success and start to visualise the business that you'd like to build:

How many days/hours would you like to work in your coaching business?

Will you be working from home, alone or with others?

How do you feel about group programs as well as 1:1 work?

What level of income do you aspire to earn?

What excites you?

CHAPTER SUMMARY

The key learning points from this chapter include:

1. There are two core pillars of the successful and sustainable coaching business model:
2. The business is built through community online using attraction marketing.
3. The business is built from a portfolio of services.
4. The core concept of attraction marketing is that you consistently create and share highly valuable content that you know your prospective clients can benefit from.
5. Creating a ladder of services where people can join you at different levels of investment will help you to serve more clients who want and need your support and enable you to grow and scale your business.

BUILDING COMMUNITIES

"At the crux of this strategy is one simple business rule: In order to get clients, they need to know that you exist"

— *JO WHEATLEY & ZOE HAWKINS*

Building communities is all about relationship building, so if you're good at building relationships you're going to enjoy this part of building your coaching business and the good news is you can start now! Coaching is focused on building relationships that enable people to express their authentic true selves. The work we do with our clients starts before they are paying for our services. You will be helping your potential clients to feel seen and heard through the content you share, and the way you interact and show up. Being able to build relationships at scale is what creates community, and when you master bringing people together and enabling them to feel welcome and heard, you have a pool of people who trust you enough that they will want to invest in your services, and you in return, will help them to achieve their goals. It's a win – win, which is really what business is about.

At the crux of this strategy of building business through community is one simple business rule - in order to get clients, they need to know that you exist. Building communities is about raising your visibility so people can get to know you and your values and then decide if you are a good fit for them. It sounds obvious but it's often overlooked - after all, being visible often awakens the inner critic. For you to create a successful coaching business your clients have to know, like and trust you and the only way they can do that is if you are visible and show them what is special about working with you. There are lots of ways you can do this, all underpinned by communities that you want to be part of. This ensures that your energy is positive and you enjoy investing time in growing and nurturing the relationships.

Connection is an innate human need; we all have a desire to be in relationships. When you create a community that people want to be a part of, they will come to spend time, build relationships with you and invite others to come and join in too. Your community becomes a huge asset, full of loyal followers who are interested in what you are talking about as well as buying from you. As ideal clients of yours, they also become your focus group to socialise new ideas. This is how we created our Coaching Crowd Business Lounge. In our free Facebook community, The Coaching Crowd, we noticed a pattern in posts in the group about wanting to know how to build a successful coaching business. We suggested the idea of a paid membership to help coaches with starting and developing a coaching business and there was a high level of interest. We invited everyone that was interested to a focus group and designed the key elements of the Business Lounge from what the focus group asked for. You get to listen and be part of rich conversations in your communities which tell you about the needs your clients have. This enables you to offer services that your prospective clients are ready to buy.

Communities are your place and so you can be authentically you within them. You create the rules, so you can feel safe there. They also nurture a sense of purpose that can resource you with energy, provide positive momentum and create impact. It's a heart led activity, but also a useful sales strategy and as coaches we must not shy away from activities that engage sales. Sales mean service and service means positive impact.

If you choose to build a community as part of your coaching business, build it with your ideal client in mind. You create a space that meets their values and is tailored to their needs. The core questions you'll consider before you build your community are:

- WHO – Who is your ideal client?
- VALUE – What do they value?
- WHERE – Where do they hang out?
- NEED - What do they need?

You'll start exploring all of these questions as you continue to progress through this book. For now, we'll explore five options for building communities that we have engaged with and that have created positive results in our business. You can choose to build your community anywhere that brings you the most joy and where your ideal clients like to spend time. You don't need to use all five of these. Find one that ignites excitement in you and can be the start for your community based coaching business.

1. LinkedIn

> "When it's time for you to embrace your business as a coach, your network is there, ready to support you"
>
> — *ZOE HAWKINS & JO WHEATLEY*

LinkedIn is the world's largest professional networking platform and is a great place to connect with and grow an audience of your prospective clients. The useful thing about LinkedIn is that you can proactively find, connect with and join in the conversations of your ideal clients, building relationships as you go. Once you are clear on your ideal client you can begin adding them to your network. Then, using your profile, you can also share valuable content in your posts or through articles that you believe your connections will enjoy engaging with. It's a way to share your message and build your brand proactively.

The more you post, the more of your network will get to see what you have to say. Even if you have a network with over 5000 connections, only a small slice of that network will see each piece of content. The more you use the platform, engage with your network and join conversations that are taking place, the more people in your network will see you and get to know you. Plus, it's not just your network that have the opportunity to get to know you, the connections of your network will also get shown your content when they interact with you, so it's a great way to share your message with the world. There are lots of features on LinkedIn that support professional networking, such as events and live video and it's a platform that is constantly developing to support people to connect with others.

Growing a community on LinkedIn starts with growing your network and this is something you can start now while you are getting ready to launch your business. Some things you can do now to support you with setting up a successful and sustainable coaching business are:

1. Update your profile and your bio
2. Connect daily with ideal clients
3. Start to post regularly about topics you are passionate about and are of value to your ideal coaching client
4. Engage in conversations that take your interest

If you'd like to come and connect with us, please do! Let us know you've found us through this book, we always look forward to meeting new community members!

https://www.linkedin.com/in/joannewheatley/

https://www.linkedin.com/in/zoehawkinscoach/

Once you decide to undertake accredited coach training, we advise you to post about the fact you have just signed up to coach training. Share the emotions you feel and the reasons for doing the training. Bring your audience on the journey with you. Then, as you complete each bit of learning or practice, post about what you learnt from it, how you felt, tag your fellow trainees, talk about the impact for you now and in the future. You can also showcase testimonials from your practice clients. All of these actions, on a regular basis, keep you front of mind for coaching. When it's time for you to embrace your business as a coach, your network is there, ready to support you. All of these actions give you a head start and when you do this consistently, you're likely to find people messaging you to enquire about working with you.

2. Facebook Groups

> "Facebook is the after conference party"
>
> — ZOE HAWKINS & JO WHEATLEY

If LinkedIn is the professional network, Facebook is the after conference party. When people are on Facebook they are often there with a 'social hat' on. Facebook Groups are a place to 'gather together' prospective clients and create communities that are more informal and relaxed, whilst still providing value. As the leader of your Facebook group, your role is to encourage conversations and connection as well as sharing content that is of value to your group members.

When you first open and start a Facebook group, it can feel like you are talking to no-one. It takes time and effort to grow the community and for people to feel relaxed and safe to share, ask questions and contribute. Facebook Groups tend to take on a life of their own when they reach around 1000 members. Whilst this may feel like a stretch now, you'll see how possible it is through the content strategy we share with you at the end of this chapter.

It's important to maintain perspective whilst growing your Facebook Group. If you were in a room with ten people and you had a chance to engage and build relationship with those ten people, knowing that they liked and were interested in what you had to say, you'd be excited by that. This is what a Facebook group is. It's a virtual room and whether you have ten or ten thousand people with you, the focus is on relationship building and adding value.

Here are some of the ways you can set up, grow and nurture a Facebook group.

1. Create a compelling name that attracts your ideal clients
2. Be active in your group, sharing content, posing questions and replying to any comments
3. Hold a Facebook Live every week sharing a valuable topic

4. Invite guests who have complimentary audiences to interview in your group
5. Run competitions to increase members
6. Create polls and ask questions about what your group would find valuable
7. Invite people from your other networks (i.e., LinkedIn) to join you in your group
8. Be consistent, show up regularly and consistently

Facebook obviously isn't the only platform to create a virtual community on. With technology developing at such a rapid pace, there are always new platforms emerging where communities can be built, so there are many others that you can choose from, including Instagram, Mighty Networks, Slack – the list is long and ever growing. We're sharing Facebook with you as that is where we have had success with our Coaching Crowd group. Find one that suits you and who you want to work with and start there.

LinkedIn, Facebook and other similar communities are easily accessible, but the one drawback is that you do not own the platform and so you are subject to the rules and regulations of a third party. If you adhere to the platform rules, it's unlikely you'll get removed, but if all of your communities are built on third party platforms there is a risk that you could lose all the relationships that you have worked hard to create. Therefore, you need to consider how to mitigate against this.

3. YouTube

> "*Share valuable content and establish yourself as an expert in your field, by appealing to multiple senses*"
>
> — *ZOE HAWKINS & JO WHEATLEY*

YouTube is another platform on which you can build a community, share valuable content and establish yourself as an expert in your field. Creating video content appeals to multiple senses. As well as learning what you have to say, viewers get to see you and hear you in action, they get to feel like they know you. By subscribing to your channel, viewers will get alerted to new content you release so they can return to your videos time and time again. The key is to create and share content regularly so that viewers keep wanting more and more and can rely on your as a source of learning that they want to engage in. Once you get to a certain level of subscribers you can monetise your channel too, providing you with semi passive income.

As you share your content on YouTube, you can add "Calls to Action" for your viewers to join you in your other communities, or to head to your website, a free resource you're offering, or other ways they can find out about your communities or paid services.

A YouTube channel is easy to set up and you can use the videos across your other social media platforms. We've experimented with different approaches to YouTube over the years. We've made short videos of us discussing coaching topics, demonstrating coaching tools, sharing replays of masterclasses and live recordings of our podcast show, as well as testimonials from our coaching qualification trainees and graduates. The idea for our YouTube channel came from all the lives we were doing in Facebook groups. We decided to repurpose them. It has since become a very popular way for people to find us and come and join our Coaching Crowd community.

4. Podcasts

> *"What could you talk about for hours that your ideal clients would like to hear?"*
>
> — *JO WHEATLEY & ZOE HAWKINS*

Podcasts are a popular community building tool used by coaches and entrepreneurs because listening to a podcast has a feeling of intimacy about it. It is an opportunity to learn on the go and often in bite size pieces. When you share your message through a regular podcast, you get to join your prospective client at different times throughout their day and week and they feel like you're talking to them and they get to know you. It is best to release your podcast at the same time, on a weekly basis, so you will become someone's habit, e.g., 8am on a Monday morning every week, your prospective clients start their week listening to you. If they enjoy your content and become a regular listener, they're likely to tell their colleagues about snippets that they particularly liked and recommend you to others and so your audience grows. The podcast industry is growing rapidly and people are always looking for new podcasts to listen to.

The way to use a podcast to build community is to link it up to other places that you are active. For example, at the end of a podcast episode you may invite people to download a free resource so that they join your e-mail list, or you invite them to join you inside your free Facebook Group. You may be noticing that all of these communities support one another and are a way for you to rapidly increase your visibility and scale your business!

We decided to launch our podcast "The Coaching Crowd", as a way to reach new audiences, those who prefer to digest content through purely listening. In an average week, we talk for hours about coaching anyway so we knew we'd enjoy putting some of these thoughts and conversations into a podcast. To get started, we asked our Coaching Crowd community what questions they had when they were thinking about training to become a coach and we used these as the titles of each of our episodes. It was a great way to engage our audience, show how we value them and make sure that our podcast spoke to our future audience.

When we launched our Coaching Crowd Podcast, we got to number one ranking in the UK Apple Business Careers charts on day one of our release and we achieved that through the support of our communities across our different platforms. It shows how, when you get focused and invest in something, you can achieve whatever you want to.

You can grow your podcast listeners and other communities by guesting on other people's podcasts. This gives you visibility to their audiences and as the person they know, like and trust believes in you and your services their listeners are likely to find it easy to as well. So, if creating your own podcast seems daunting right now, perhaps start with guesting as a way to let people know about your other communities.

If you're thinking a podcast would be an enjoyable way for you to create community, have think about what you could talk about for hours that your ideal clients would like to hear?

5. In Person Groups And Networks

> *"A great way for you to establish your expertise and brilliant if you enjoy physical interaction and like being in the energy of others"*
>
> — *ZOE HAWKINS & JO WHEATLEY*

All of the community options so far have been online and distance options, but in person groups and networks remain a great way for you to establish your expertise and they are brilliant if you enjoy being in the physical energy of others. When you make connections in these spaces you can invite people to join your online communities to develop your relationship further. You can support your in-person community with online methods too, such as the Facebook group or email.

Once you have decided what area of coaching you want to work in, you can design a group and start inviting people to it. This might be a monthly networking meet up of people who share similar interests, it could be a regular breakfast or lunch meeting that you host where you share different topics or host guest speakers, you might even choose to wrap in other interests such as running or walking and create groups which blend an activity with your specific coaching approach. The point is that you can be creative about the ways to connect and create community. There are no rules. You get to decide and test out what works for you and your ideal clients.

REFLECTION QUESTIONS

As we draw this chapter to a close, let's finish with some questions for you to reflect on to help you define your thoughts on building business through community:

Which of the communities mentioned so far bring you excitement and curiosity?

What other ideas do you have for communities as part of your coaching business?

CHAPTER SUMMARY

The key learning points from this chapter include:

1. Creating communities and sharing compelling, valuable content within them, is a great way to build a stable foundation for a coaching business.

2. Communities can be created in lots of different places, for example LinkedIn, Facebook and You Tube.

3. When you create a community, make sure you're creating one that you want to be a part of so that your energy is positive and aligned to the community's purpose.

4. Create a community that your ideal client will want to be part of.

COMMUNICATING THROUGH CONTENT

"Your content is what will help you to establish yourself as an expert in your niche and draw clients into your communities like a magnet"

— *ZOE HAWKINS & JO WHEATLEY*

C ommunities become a source of clients when they are engaged, active and interested in what you have to offer. Like all relationships, you have to work at getting to know people and doing this at scale is an important aspect of building a successful and sustainable coaching business. Once you have chosen and created your communities, you'll need communicate and interact with them so you can nurture trusting relationships. One way you can do that is through creating and sharing compelling content, that is highly valuable and helps your ideal clients begin to make progress with the very thing they're in your community for. In this chapter, we'll share with you how to communicate through compelling content so your community grows, remains engaged and interested in what you have to offer and ultimately wants to buy your services. We'll share the strategy and the practicalities of applying this.

We'll start with content strategy. A content strategy is the backbone of your community and the central part to attraction marketing. It's how you'll show your ideal clients the depth of your knowledge, skill and expertise. Your content is what will help you to establish yourself firmly within your niche as the 'go–to' expert and draw clients into your communities like a magnet, hence the term attraction marketing. It relies on you sharing highly valuable content on a regular basis. We recommend weekly, but if that feels too much at first, you could choose an alternative duration and start there. The most important element is that whatever you do, you do it consistently.

There is a compound effect to growing and communicating with your community. The more people that see your content the more they share with others how valuable it is. If you do this one thing consistently, over time your communities will grow in both number and engagement. Consistency, perseverance and patience are required.

We know it can feel overwhelming to think about creating regular content so we're going to break it down for you so you can see how communities and content work together to create the foundation of your coaching business.

An effective attraction marketing strategy is built from four core actions:

1. Creating weekly content
2. Sharing that content within the community you create
3. Re-purposing your content in multiple ways
4. Adding people to your communities

The first thing to do is to choose a medium of content that you would enjoy sharing every week. Remember earlier we shared that this could be:

- A blog
- A top-tips email bulletin
- A podcast
- An educational video

You may have other ideas to add to this. You can batch your content so you are not having to create content every week. We tend to set aside a day per month to batch a number of podcasts for the month ahead. It could be done once a quarter. You might be wondering how you can come up with content for each week, but you'll be surprised how easily this can come to you when you put your mind to it and step into the shoes of your ideal client. An approach that works for many people is breaking the year down into weekly themes and creating content around each theme. For example, if you're a coach who is passionate about self-care, throughout January you may choose to focus on new routines and goals for wellness, given that January is often a month associated with new beginnings.

This may look like:

Week 1 – Self-care goals for the year

Week 2 – How to maintain momentum

Week 3 – Establishing new routines

Week 4 – Celebrating new habits

As you move into February you might choose to spotlight different aspects of self-care for example:

Week 5 – Stress Management

Week 6 – Managing self care through change

Week 7 – Sleep habits

Week 8 – Emotional regulation

If you find yourself struggling to come up with ideas at certain points you can go to your community and ask them what they'd like to hear about.

Once you have some good ideas for content, you can release a piece of content each week. i.e. a podcast episode or a blog whichever is your preferred way to engage with your community. Then, you'll re-purpose that content by sharing it across your communities. For example, if you have a podcast that's released weekly, you share your podcast episode on LinkedIn and in your Facebook group. On your podcast episode itself, you invite people to join you in your Facebook group or connect with you on LinkedIn. Each community feeds the other so that you increase your chances of being in front of your ideal clients exactly when they need you.

You also take this one step further by posting each day of the week, talking about a particular element of your theme that week. In this way one piece of content becomes your social media plan and content for the week. This provides a clear plan.

As well as sharing content within your communities, you'll need to continually grow your community so that you aren't just talking to the same people over and over. You can do this through activities we shared in the previous chapter, for example adding people on LinkedIn and inviting them to your Facebook group. There are also other strategies you can use here such as:

- Engaging in complimentary Facebook Groups
- Maximising your SEO
- Paid advertising services
- Engaging with influencers to support you

There are many ways you can grow your community and like all professions, the more you put into it, the more you learn. The most important step is to start! You don't need complicated strategies or a deep pocket for advertising to start growing a community. Pick one community, one form of content and layer it up from there. Over time, you will see that all your small efforts amount into a significant presence and brand. We see people in our Coaching Crowd Business

Lounge starting out every day, having and sharing their successes. We all grow together.

Now that you know how to create content and communicate with your community, we need to consider how it is shared and a primary place for this is your e-mail list.

Building your email list is an important part of business because this is the one thing you will own. It's the central place that brings all of your communities together. Having an email list gives you an opportunity to communicate with your ideal clients on a regular basis, keeping you front of mind and whilst many people's e-mail inboxes are busy, if your content strategy is working and designed around your ideal clients' needs, the people who join your email list are going to learn to look out for your emails and make time to read them.

There are two stages to building an email list. The first is getting people onto your email list and the second is emailing them regularly them once they are there.

One of the fastest ways to grow your email list is to create what is known as a 'lead magnet'. A lead magnet is a valuable resource that you make available to prospective clients in exchange for their e-mail address. Examples include:

1. Free 'how to' guides
2. Checklists
3. Quizzes
4. Masterclasses
5. Videos or video series
6. Brochures

7. Templates

Your lead magnet can be whatever you want it to be, and it's best designed by looking through the eyes of your prospective clients and the resources they're looking for to help them to solve their problem, which is their pain point. We created a lead magnet which is a quiz, helping prospective clients to answer the question 'which coaching course is right for me?'. We created it because it's a question we get asked often as coaching trainers. You can take a look as an example here - www.mycoachingcourse.com. We have people completing this quiz daily to help them to decide what coaching course to do. They provide their email so that they can be sent the results of the quiz. Those results include a video from us about the course they are best matched to as well as brochures for our training programmes. They get the option to be sent the results or also be added to our wider e-mail list for regular content. It is essential that you follow the data protection regulations in your country. Being ethical in your coaching practice and business is fundamental to your reputation.

Your lead magnet might be one of your most popular pieces of content that you've already put out. Or it might be a resource that builds on a free piece of content. You can embed your lead magnet into your blog posts, educational videos, social media posts and within your community to continually encourage more people to join your email list.

If you're thinking "what would I email them?", then this is where your content strategy comes in. You'll be emailing your subscribers, each week when you release your weekly content, sharing with them highlights from the latest piece and linking to it so they have easy access to read it. Whilst your subscribers may be in one of your other communities, you can't rely on them seeing it, or seeing it at a time that's convenient for them. Having it in their inbox means that they can choose when to open your email and take a look at the latest release.

Your content strategy means that you will never be out of reasons to email your subscribers, and as you're sharing regular, valuable content with them, you can also embed ways your clients can work with you onto those regular emails. This way, when clients are ready to work with you, they know exactly how to do that. You can also use your email list to support you when you are launching new services or offering new coaching packages.

Your subscribers won't always open your emails but seeing you in their inbox regularly keeps you front and centre of their mind. It's normal practice in the coaching industry to email your list weekly, some people do more. The key is to find out what works for your audience and to test different email formats and see what gets the most engagement. Being prepared to learn and adapt is fundamental to success.

Lastly, perspective is important because it's not the size of the email list or community that is important, but the number of people on it who engage with you. A small list can lead to more clients than a huge list. It's how you serve your clients that is important. Serve them well and your email and client list will grow. When you have thousands of contacts, show up for them in the same way as if you're building a relationship with one special person.

REFLECTION QUESTIONS

As we draw this chapter to a close, let's finish with some questions for you to reflect on to help you connect with how you would like to communicate with your communities:

What ideas has this sparked in you?

Which of the mediums for content excite you most?

What ideas do you have of your own?

CHAPTER SUMMARY

The key learning points in this chapter include:

1. Creating compelling content underpins community building and is something that will take dedicated time and focus in business.
2. Your content strategy enables you to take one piece of content and turn it into a week's worth of engaging posts and information.
3. Building an email list is an important part of building a sustainable coaching business because it's the one community you fully own.

PORTFOLIO OF SERVICES

"Taking a learner and growth mindset to your coaching business will help you to embrace the reality that your business is a living, organic system and is naturally seeking to evolve"

— *JO WHEATLEY & ZOE HAWKINS*

The options for using your coaching training are vast and people are creative with how they use their coaching skills and qualification to create a business that uses the full range of their skills and strengths. Social media and online platforms enable us all to create businesses that have the flexibility to grow and adapt. When you reach the point of designing your business, our hope is that you gain inspiration and ideas from this chapter on how you can structure your business to make the most of your new talents. In this chapter, we will share with you some elements that can be pillars in your portfolio of coaching services.

Having a portfolio of services means that you have different income streams in your business, so if one is affected by market changes or your ill health for example, you have the stability and resilience from another. Having a range of services in your business means that you spread the risk and increase the potential for reward. Another reason why the portfolio business model is important is because there's a ceiling to the number of 1:1 clients you can work with as a coach and therefore a ceiling to your income and those you can help. 1:1 coaching can be hugely rewarding and can provide a good level of income, but when you are ready to grow and scale, you can only do that through raising your prices, if you stick to the 1:1 business model. Many coaches also reach a point where they want to increase the impact that they are having in the world and leave a bigger legacy by supporting as many clients as possible. So, given the compelling reasons for having a portfolio of services, let's explore what this could look like by considering three approaches.

1. Integrating Coaching With Other Expertise

Offering coaching alongside your other areas of expertise, such as HR, marketing, sales consultancy etc., is a great way to transition into a coaching career. In this model, you will have your consultancy services as an offer as well as coaching and one will feed and add value to the other. When we began In Good Company, our very first piece of work was designing 'leadership and management essentials' e-learning content for a well known online training provider. It was combining our HR expertise with our coaching approach. It began to build our confidence.

In the early days in our business, we were known best for our HR experience and so we reached out to our network and offered our leadership development services which led to us being commissioned by a global organisation to design a leadership development programme for IT leaders. Our design and facilitation of this programme led to us being shortlisted for Best Learning and Development Supplier by the Chartered Institute of Personnel and Development. 1:1 coaching was part of the design of the programme to support the group facilitation, and the content of the leadership programme itself was built upon coaching principles. This programme built our reputation as coaches as well as leadership development experts and as our business evolved, our confidence and reputation as coaches grew and we stepped more fully into the coaching side of our work.

Where you start in business is not where you will necessarily be one, three, five, even ten years from now, so the portfolio can grow and change in terms of balance and direction based on what's needed and what you enjoy delivering.

Here are some reflection questions you might find useful as you consider what services you could offer alongside coaching:

- What elements of your current expertise would you enjoy bringing into your coaching business?
- How can your current expertise help you to get coaching clients?
- How important is it for you to maintain your current expertise?
- How could this approach help you to nurture your current network who hold you in high regard?
- Would this make it easier for your network to recommend you?

2. One To Many Offers

Building on this, a second option for creating a portfolio of services is to create a one-to-many coaching offering to add to your 1:1 coaching services. Many coaches add a 'one-to-many' element to their work as a way to enable them to support a greater number of clients. One-to-many basically means you are the 'one' and you provide your services to 'many' people all in one go, for example, through group programmes or courses. Whilst many coaches wait to add this to their offering, we recommend adding it into your business model from the beginning.

Let's take a look at four options for one-to-many offerings to help you understand more about what they are and to help you connect with whether they may form a part of your coaching business strategy.

Courses

You may choose to create a course as part of your one-to-many offering. A course is where you would help your clients to solve a problem they have through a programme you facilitate. It may be a programme you teach live, it may be pre-recorded and self study, or a blend of the two. You can support your learners with workbooks and other resources. You may also choose to incorporate elements of 1:1 within your courses too. Designing your course can be fun and you can be creative with it! There are no rules, you'll know your clients' needs best and you get to design it with those in mind as well as your own.

We became coach trainers, in part, because so many of our clients started commenting on how powerful coaching was for them and how they'd like to learn more about how to coach. Adding coaching training to our portfolio of services was transformational for our business and has enabled us to serve many more clients than we ever could through 1:1 alone. Today, we find many HR people come and train with us because of our strong and credible background in HR. We also run in-house workshops, which are bite size pieces of coaching topics and we can we re-purpose this content to sell on our website through our shop, meaning that there are more ways for our clients to access our impactful and tried and tested work.

Think back to the expertise you are bringing from your career. There are likely hundreds of things you could share with others. Perhaps you are bringing experience from recruiting and could create a course in values-based recruitment, or maybe you have a lot of experience in managing your own mental health and wellbeing and could create a programme for others on how to prioritise their self-care. The options are endless. The key is ensuring that your clients want what you have to offer and you can find this out by getting out there and speaking with your potential clients to really understand their needs. Focus groups are a great way to do this.

Group Coaching Programmes

Group coaching programmes can be a great way to offer a lower, more accessible financial entry point for clients, when compared to 1:1 coaching. A group coaching programme is typically working with a small number of clients in one go and facilitating live sessions for them in a semi structured fashion.

It is different from a course because you work with the emerging needs of the group, bringing different coaching tools and activities to each session. There is a lot of skill involved in group coaching because it requires you to create very high trust amongst group members and to proactively manage the group dynamics to maintain group safety. It's a format that will draw heavily on your coaching skills and be hugely rewarding for group participants. There is enormous value in shared learning spaces because clients begin to see that they are not alone in the challenges they face and their learning is accelerated through the support of the group as well as watching and learning how other group members respond and adapt to their challenges.

Membership

A membership is essentially a subscription service where members pay a monthly subscription to be part of a group and receive support and guidance for a need that is common to all members. Whereas a course provides a linear solution, guiding learners from point a to point b, a membership is typically more ad hoc and provides learning content based on needs. For example, in The Coaching Crowd Business Lounge, each month we invite an industry expert to come and join us to talk about an aspect of growing a coaching business. Topics have included copywriting, branding, growing an email list, using Facebook Groups, accounting basics for coaches etc. All the topics are relevant to growing a coaching business. Members dive in and out of content as they need it, depending on which point of business they are at. We have support and accountability pods, an online group platform to ask questions and get advice and we host live and recorded Q&A sessions every month where the membership get to spend time with us drawing on our experience. It also gives us the chance, as hosts, to get to know our members more closely. One of the things members love is that it's purely for people building coaching businesses, rather than all types of aspiring entrepreneurs, so everyone understands the nuances of setting up and growing a coaching business.

Most memberships are community based, meaning that a lot of the value in being in a membership is the mutual support and wisdom of the members. Many memberships are supported by private collaboration spaces, where members can have conversations, network, ask questions and receive feedback on their ideas.

The good thing about a membership is it can provide a stable recurring base income each month, giving you a level of predictability around your cash flow. Of course, you will see members leave as they outgrow the group, but you can also launch your membership at different times throughout the year to encourage new members to sign up, even if it is open for new members to join at any time throughout the year. A launch brings eyes onto your service.

Memberships can also be really fulfilling for the host. As a coach, working independently can be lonely. Running a community like a membership can be rewarding and engaging, because it is a place you can go to build relationships and join conversations.

Live Masterclasses

Live Masterclasses are sessions you host where you take attendees through highly valuable expert content in a class that lasts usually somewhere between one to two hours. The best ones are usually interactive and value packed, where attendees get to engage with you through the chat function or conversing with you live, and the session usually involves some kind of interactive activity – as opposed to just one way teaching.

Over the years, we have run a range of Masterclasses on topics such as an Introduction to Coaching, Emotions Coaching, Values, Overcoming Limiting Belief... the options are endless and again, it's where you can be creative and share content on topics you enjoy talking about.

Masterclasses can be free or paid. Where you offer them for free, they are a great way to build your audience and engage with your community. Where they are paid, it's a great offer to add to your portfolio of services and it can be easily scaled.

The great thing about masterclasses is that you can re-purpose the content for other means. For example, if you run a paid masterclass, you can record it, turn it into a mini course and offer it for sale on your website, therefore creating another way to serve your clients and receive income.

If your masterclass is a free resource, you can record it, upload it to YouTube or a replay page on your website and use this as a free download to encourage people to join your communities.

So that's a number of different one-to-many options. Let's take a look at other ways you can build a portfolio business.

3. Associate Work

Associate work is something many coaches consider when they are starting out. This is where you work as a coach for another organisation. The associate organisation secures a contract for coaching and then engages with associates to fulfil the contract. The benefits are that you don't have to spend time on business development to secure the contract. You get paid for the hours of work you complete on behalf of the organisation and you often have the benefit of flexibility in your diary management. Some associate coaching organisations also provide learning and development support. Working in this way can provide a regular and reliable source of income as you build your own coaching business.

Be conscious that when you are busy working in someone else's business, it can be hard to build your own brand or get testimonials for your work, because often, your work as an associate needs to remain confidential under the associate organisation.

Working as an associate coach often requires you to undergo a rigorous recruitment process that likely has a number of stages. The foundational requirements are usually a coaching qualification and that you are accredited with a coaching body such as the European Mentoring and Coaching Council, International Coach Federation or the Association of Coaching.

Here are some questions you might like to reflect on to help you when considering this approach to your coaching business:

1. Are my values aligned to doing associate work?
2. How do I feel about not building my own coaching business brand?
3. Is there a minimum commitment of hours required per week?
4. What is the resignation period?

5. What is the hourly pay and how does it compare to what I will charge as a coach in my own right?
6. Is there access to the other associate coaches that I could benefit from?
7. Do they offer training and development opportunities?
8. What are the confidentiality terms?

The business model you design will evolve over the years and in fact, it needs to evolve in order to stay current and thrive. Taking a learner and growth mindset to your coaching business will help you to embrace the reality that your business is a living, organic system and is naturally seeking to evolve. Be open to sensing where it wants to go next. Just as you are now with your career!

REFLECTION QUESTIONS

As we draw this chapter to a close, let's finish with some questions for you to reflect on to help you consider how a portfolio approach to your coaching business could work well:

What excites me about a portfolio business model?

What services come to mind that I would enjoy offering?

What other skills and expertise might I blend with my coaching skills?

CHAPTER SUMMARY

The key learning points in this chapter include:

1. A portfolio business is a coaching business that has a range of services available, such as 1:1 coaching and one-to-many offers too.
2. There are many ways to blend coaching with existing skills and start out offering consultancy, or working as an associate to other organisations.
3. A portfolio of services provides resilience and opportunities to grow with your clients' needs.

STARTING OUT

> "Exploring the option of going into partnership with others can be useful to consider up front"
>
> — JO WHEATLEY & ZOE HAWKINS

In coaching, there is a lot of focus on beginnings and endings and how to navigate them successfully. Coaches encourage clients to start with the end in mind and building a business is no different. In the previous chapters, we outlined ways to structure your business in terms of services. In this chapter, we're going to explore the reality of starting out so you take time to strategically plan your first moves based on what you'd like to achieve. We'll help you to think ahead about decisions of whether to go into business with someone else or go it alone, and where to invest when starting out.

One of the questions on people's minds when they think about transitioning into the role of coach is whether they'll find it lonely. Having been employed and been part of teams and leading projects, it can feel daunting to leave that behind to go it alone, so exploring the option of going into partnership with others can be useful to consider up front. The decision for us to go into partnership has been a great fit for us, and as strong as our partnership is, being in business with someone isn't a decision to take lightly.

We met on day one of our HR Masters at Plymouth university in 2001. We had known and supported each other for ten years after that, as friends and peers, before we formed In Good Company. We supported each other throughout our HR careers and were each others' confidant and professional sounding board, even though we worked in different sectors and organisations. Having had such a strong friendship, we knew we had similar values and beliefs and respected the skills and qualities we brought to our work. We think in a similar way and each of us bring a different perspective too, which adds value. We have seen each other through the ups and downs of life and therefore knew one another at our strongest and weakest. Our coaching training gave us the confidence that our shared values could be served by working together, so we took a coaching approach to our decision making and have built our business partnership through strong contracting and relationship building.

When we chose to set up a coaching business together it enabled us to feel more confident about the decision. We also genuinely wanted to share in the joy of the learning experience. We wanted to have someone to celebrate with and to create with and someone to keep the faith if the other was having a wobble. It was the best decision we made. We will be forever grateful for the connection we have and all that we have achieved through our relationship. Like all relationships, it takes attention and needs to be nurtured and we learn and grow through that too, for the benefit of us and all of our relationships.

In a business partnership, you bring your creative ideas, your passion and thirst for driving your business forward. These ideas will not always be in total alignment with your business partner's. We are highly skilled at sitting in the creative tension we experience when neither one of us is having their ideas accepted by the other. We know, through experience, that on the other side of that tension is an even better, more aligned idea. We accept, manage and appreciate each others' needs. We have safe space in our relationship to be emotionally honest and have the container to facilitate all the emotions that we experience. We make conscious choices to support each other and in doing so, our business grows too. Our coaching training provided us with a deep appreciation and understanding of human behaviour and we're able to apply that to our ways of working.

There are many benefits to forming a business partnership, including having two creative and strategic brains, two networks to draw from, someone to share the unique experience with. It can also add a level of complexity that isn't there when you are working on your own. Here are some questions that can help you to reflect on what a business partnership may mean for you:

1. Do you enjoy having someone to share things with?
2. How do you feel about sharing the profits?
3. How will being in a business partnership alter your other relationships?
4. How would you navigate exiting the business partnership if one of you wanted to leave at a different time to the other?
5. What are the legal considerations of working with someone?
6. Do you want to build a personal brand more than a company brand?
7. Who could you potentially go into business with?
8. What would entering a partnership add to your decision making?

If there aren't obvious people in your support circle right now that you'd think about going into business with, you may find that opportunity presents itself as you journey into coaching. We often see partnerships coming out of our coaching trainings. Not necessarily from people on the same cohort, but when people have undertaken the same deep-rooted coaching training and made the decision to train with the same provider, there is a connection, a respect and a kinship that can provide a strong foundation for a relationship.

For many years, our sole brand was In Good Company, but we also stand in our own identities as coaches with our own personal brand, coaching packages and websites, so it is possible, of course, to have a hybrid.

You may not have thought this far yet. There are many benefits to setting up your coaching business on your own. You get the freedom to make all the decisions, be creative, take rapid action on your ideas and really test yourself. You get to become known for what you do and be an expert in your field, you can also build a support network around you and choose to collaborate with others for defined projects or ideas. As with all things in coaching, the choice is yours, and isn't something you have to decide to do now. Trust in the process that as you train as a coach, you'll gain a deeper understanding of your needs.

Having spent some time reflecting on whether you'd go into business with someone or not, let's look at some of the practical aspects of where you may want to invest your time and money in the early days of starting out. We'll consider branding, professional photography and website.

Branding

People buy people. Your branding is an extension of you and reflects who you are and how you do business. At the start of doing business you may not be sure what your branding needs to represent, and that's ok. The process of developing your branding helps to clarify your message, and your branding will continue to evolve as you do.

Looking back, our early branding didn't really reflect us; it was bold and brash, the imagery we used was corny and didn't tell a story, our logo was also clearly DIY. You could argue that it didn't entirely hold us back because we had lots of success in the first seven years of business. However, when we invested in professional branding our business started to really fly because we were able to tell a story, not just with the words we were using but with the imagery, colours and brand we were showcasing. We were consistent and it had depth. Branding gives a sense of pride in who you are and the services you provide. It is your signature and it becomes familiar to people.

People communicate in many different ways and visuals are an important part of connection. Great branding helps to bring you and your services to life in an aligned way. If your branding doesn't resonate with your clients, it may be enough to stop them investing in you and your services.

When you're starting out, we highly recommend you budget for professional branding, so you can bring alive who you are and what you do in a way which will resonate with your clients.

Your branding can also help elevate other things you choose to do yourself. For example, if you build your website yourself but you have invested in your branding, the overall look of your website is going to be more professional than DIY.

Professional Photography

Another area we recommend investing in is professional photography. Similar to branding, your clients want to get to know you before investing in your services and photography is one way they're going to do that. When your photography is aligned to your branding you are building a cohesive and reliable brand for your clients to invest in.

You need high quality images that you can use for your website, PR and promotional materials. They will show that you invest in yourself. There is always a place for casual photography, but it's not on your website. Casual photography can be used to engage clients through social media, but when it comes to the face of your business, it's important to have photography that aligns to your brand and the image that you want to portray.

We subscribe to a quarterly photoshoot now so it is prioritised and we can plan images that match our business activity. It's something that has become enjoyable and we use the day for business strategy as well.

Website

You don't have to have a website to get started. Many clients will be engaging with you on social media and within your communities long before they visit your website and you can advertise your services through your social media pages. That said, websites are helpful in showing your clients more details about who you are and what you have to offer. Their main function now is a place for people to purchase your services and where you can provide them with terms and conditions of what is and isn't included in your services. A well built website can also enable you to use it to support other activities such as blogging, vlogging and general SEO purposes.

Creating a website can be a time vortex that can absorb many valuable days and months from your getting started plan! You have to know when to stop editing and changing and move onto the next activity. Progress over perfection. If you have invested in branding and photography, all you really need next is a simple three page website – a 'Home Page', A 'Services Page' and a 'Contact Page'. Everything else can be added at a later date, as you refine your message, coaching packages and approach.

To get a website up and running you need:

1. A domain name – you can purchase a domain name from any reputable domain name provider. We use Ionos, for no other reason than it was the first one we came across!
2. Hosting – You will need a service that hosts your website. Many of the domain name providers or website builders offer this too.

You have two choices when it comes to creating a website. Build it yourself, or get a professional to do it for you. If quick and simple is your thing you can find many online website builders that enable you to build your own website. We started with a Wix website. You may also want to take a look at the website builders that come with whoever you choose your hosting with.

The reason quick and simple is often a good idea in the early days is because it may take time to understand your needs and what you want your website to do. As your business and ideas expand, your requirements will change. So having a simple website in the outset is a bit like taking a car for a test drive. Work out what you like and don't like and build out your specifications from there.

With a simple three page website, once you have your branding and photography, even the most technologically inexperienced coach can build a compelling website – if you want to! It's not something everyone enjoys so know that you also have the option to outsource this and save yourself both time and potentially stress!

As your needs grow and you reach a point where you are launching your services and taking bookings online here are some website features that you may find yourself needing:

1. Landing pages to take registrations to events
2. Email service provider integration so you can communicate with your registrants and potential clients through email
3. Contact forms that enable you to easily capture peoples' information
4. Online booking facility with diary integration so people can book coaching sessions with you from your website

5. Payment facility so payment can be taken directly from your website

6. Pop up messages so you can attract attention from website visitors as they navigate the pages of your website

All of these features are widely available and can often be integrated into the free website builders, sometimes at a cost. You could hire someone to build a website for you.

Another option is also to invest in an 'all in one' website platform that integrates website builder, hosting, email, landing pages, event registrations, online payment, online courses and memberships and more. We now use one of these called "Kajabi". We find it very intuitive and easy to use. For us, Kajabi saves us an enormous amount of time and money as we do not have to spend on developers every time we need to do something or change something.

If you're setting out and you want to try it for free, you can use our affiliate referral code here: https://app.kajabi.com/r/uaAnLj22

There are pro's and con's to doing things yourself or outsourcing the project to an expert. Your decision will likely be based on your technical ability, patience, time available and cost.

Our overall message to you here is have clear goals about what you want your website to do for you and know that it's OK to start with something basic. You can build on your website as you become clearer about your needs and at that point, you may choose to invest more.

Had we known years ago what we know now, we would have started out with an all-in-one platform. With the versatility it brings it would have saved us time and money. If you know that you're going to be running group programmes, launching services, hosting online events and you plan to scale quickly towards this, we recommend checking out an all-in-one platform, such as Kajabi, as it is likely to serve you best over the years.

REFLECTION QUESTIONS

As we draw this chapter to a close, let's finish with some questions for you to reflect on to help you define how want to start your coaching business:

How do I feel about going into business on my own vs a business partnership?

What do I want to note down and remember for when I am starting out?

CHAPTER SUMMARY

The key learning points in this chapter include:

1. When starting out in business there are some important decisions to be made, such as whether to go into business alone, or to go into partnership.

2. It can be tempting to do everything yourself in business when starting out but like any business, there are investment decisions to be made.

3. The three important 'starting out' activities we recommend are to invest in branding, professional photography and – if you choose to scale quickly – an all in one website solution.

NICHING

> *"Niching isn't about excluding people, it's about helping people to find you and invest in your services with confidence"*
>
> — *JO WHEATLEY & ZOE HAWKINS*

"Niching" is a term for focusing on one specific segment of the market, rather than being a generalist and it's something that often puts prospective coaches off getting started. Generally speaking, coaches are heart led, with a desire to help everyone. Excluding people from accessing your services can feel in conflict with what you're trying to achieve in the world, but niching isn't about excluding people, it's about helping people to find you and invest in your services with confidence.

The thinking is that the more specific you are with your coaching niche, the easier it is for your ideal clients to find you. Conversely, if you are a generalist who offers coaching to anyone or everyone, it is harder for your prospective clients to know whether you are talking directly to them or not. The principle is "If you talk to everyone, you talk to no one".

It was about seven years before we decided to focus on niching in our business. If we had our time again, we would have niched from the beginning. Like many coaches, we resisted it because we felt it contradicted our values of inclusivity. We hadn't been convinced that niching would help us to work with more clients by connecting more deeply with people we wanted to serve. We came to realise that even after you narrow down who you want to work with, many people who don't fit your niche still approach you asking if they can work with you. This discovery enabled us to feel comfortable with the approach. We realised that our collective niche was coach training.

One of the benefits of niching is it makes marketing your services easier, as you write and produce your content with one person in mind. The more specific you are about the people you want to work with and the more you tailor your messages to them, the more of them will find you. Investing in coaching is often a big decision and clients that are seeking coaching might be prone to indecision and procrastination. The clearer you can be with your messaging, the easier it will be for your prospective clients to invest.

Niching is about who you want to work with. Whilst it may feel that you'd like to coach everyone, as you gain experience, you'll find that you're drawn to coaching certain people over others and that certain people are drawn to work with you over others. When you train as a coach, you'll need to do a number of coaching hours to become qualified. We encourage learners to work with a range of clients so they can get a feel for the qualities, values, motivations, and personalities that they enjoy working with. As your experience grows, you'll start to get a feel for the clients you most enjoy working with and, importantly, who you feel you are a good match for.

Niching is a sweet spot between your coaching strengths and values, the clients' needs, and what they'll pay for, as shown in the diagram below. It's an adaptation from Igikai, which we call The Niche Map:

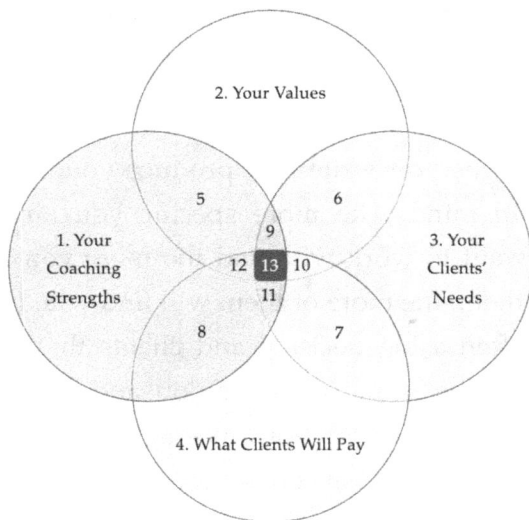

KEY:

1. Your Coaching Strengths
2. Your Values
3. Your Clients' Needs
4. What Client Will Pay
5. Your Coaching Passion
6. Your Coaching Mission
7. Your Core Message
8. Your Unique Style
9. The Clientless Coach
10. The Unfulfilled Coach
11. The Longing Coach
12. The Confused Coach
13. Your Ideal Client and Niche

Let's break this down together, looking at each part of the model in turn.

1. Your Coaching Strengths

As you build your coaching experience, you'll come to know your coaching strengths, the talents that you have that make your coaching unique. We have a super skill for pattern spotting, intuitively knowing how to help clients get in contact with what is most holding them back and helping them to overcome that rapidly. For you, it may be the speed at which you build rapport and put people at ease, or the trust you invoke in the relationship. We all have strengths when it comes to coaching and the way we combine them with our other talents makes our coaching unique.

2. Your Values

Our values guide us towards what we most enjoy in coaching. You may thrive on helping clients to set motivating actions that will enable them to move closer towards their goals, or perhaps it's enabling clients to see different perspectives and unlock greater choices. You may be drawn to these aspects of coaching because of your own values of drive or freedom.

The values that most show up in our coaching are connection, learning and freedom. We love helping clients to learn about themselves, the way they think, feel and behave. We enjoy sharing tools and resources that enable clients to self-coach, far beyond the coaching relationship, as well as paying it forward. We are motivated to help our clients find the freedom that they desire. This may be freedom from something tangible like a corporate role they no longer want to have, or intangible, such as freedom from beliefs they hold that limit them. Your values will shape the coaching experience that you offer. This could be equality, achievement, creativity for example.

3. Your Clients' Needs

Clients' needs are the intangible results that they're looking for. These are their values, their feelings, and the way they want to experience the world. For example, a client may need more inner peace from the anxiety they experience, or more joy in the way they work. Clients may need to feel a deeper connection with their loved ones, or a deeper sense of purpose in the world. Our client's needs are the things that will enrich their life.

Needs are different to goals. A goal is what the client wants to achieve, for example, you may want to leave the corporate world and set up in business as a coach, so your goal would be about training to be a coach, but your need is what is being met by achieving this goal – i.e., your need for freedom, learning, growth, or challenge.

Once a client's basic needs around safety and security are met, they start to long for their other needs to be met, such as love, belonging, self-belief and freedom, purpose and meaning. When we're coaching, we'll always be serving our clients' needs. Being clear about the needs you want to help your clients with will help you to form a clearer picture of the niche you want to target and enable you to connect with your clients' deepest desires.

4. What Clients Will Pay

You may be thinking that clients will pay to have their needs met, but that is not always the case. Clients are often more motivated by what they want than what they need. We all have needs that go unmet and it usually takes some kind of trigger for us to recognise that and to move to action to do something about it.

Let's take the example of confidence. We all need confidence. It helps us to form relationships, take risks, secure meaningful work, and enjoy social occasions, but that doesn't mean that people who experience a lack of confidence are going to pay to secure confidence. Most people find effective coping strategies to their unmet needs, and to change this can feel risky and daunting.

Following on the example, if someone experiences a lack of social confidence and this affects them by feeling shy, introverted, and keeping themselves to themselves, they are likely to develop hobbies and interests that do not require them to be the life and soul of the party. They will find and develop ways to have a small, intimate circle of friends and they learn to live comfortably in this zone, avoiding situations that may trigger the feelings associated with a lack of social confidence.

However, if this same person decides that they want to grow a business and in doing so, needs to step out of their comfort zone and build the confidence to be more visible and proactively engage with prospective clients, they are more likely to pay for the support that will enable them to develop new strategies to grow their business. What they are paying for isn't the confidence – they are paying for the ability to have a successful business.

When it comes to your prospective clients, spending time researching and understanding what they will pay for is important. You'll need to create messaging that appeals to that.

The Spaces In Between

That's the four core elements of the Niche Map covered. Let's look at the spaces in between.

5. Your Coaching Passion

Where your coaching strengths and your values intercept, this is your coaching passion. It's the place where you are working that brings you the most joy. For example, if you have core coaching strengths around building relationships and action orientation and you have values of achievement and connection, you are likely to feel deeply passionate about helping driven, ambitious individuals achieve challenging goals.

6. Your Coaching Mission

Where your values and the clients' needs intercept, this is your coaching mission. It's the place where you will feel called to help others. For example, you may have values around belonging and peace, and want to support clients who need more balance in their life. Your coaching mission may become about helping working parents to build a career that brings them both meaning and flexibility.

7. Your Core Message

Where your clients' needs and what they pay for intercept, this is the results you deliver and where you'll focus your core message. For example, if you're working with clients who need more joy and freedom in their career, and they'll pay for support in changing careers to be able to find that, you'll focus your messaging on how you help clients to successfully transition careers so that they can find more joy and meaning in their lives.

8. Your Unique Style

Where what clients will pay and your coaching strengths intercept, this is how you are unique as a coach and how you'll help your clients to see and understand how your services are different to other services available. For example, if you know your clients want to transition careers, and you have unique strengths around challenging clients expectations and supporting them with courageous action then, as you describe who you are as a coach, you might choose to draw attention to the fact that your coaching is about helping ambitious and courageous leaders confidently make life-changing decisions and you do this through challenging them to set bold actions and goals and supporting them to think bigger and more daringly than they have done before. Whereas a coach who has strengths around compassion may choose to draw on how they create safe spaces to work through the emotions and reservations that transitioning careers brings up.

So, to summarise where this takes us so far, The Niche Map enables you to consider your values, and strengths as well as your client's needs and what they'll pay for. It also helps you to consider your passion, mission, message and coaching style. The Niche Map also helps us to avoid some of the pitfalls we risk falling into when defining our niche.

The Pitfalls

Look at The Niche Map again and you'll likely notice four places on the diagram where three of the circles intersect but one does not. These areas are pitfalls that coaches risk falling into as they define their niche.

9. The Clientless Coach

The first one of these intersections is where your coaching strengths, your values and your clients' needs all intersect, but what the client will pay for isn't considered. When you're operating from this space, you'll have lots of passion for what you do, but not necessarily any clients. It may be where you excel as a coach in terms of your values, skills and how you help people, but your clients may not be willing, ready, or able to part with their money to invest in your services.

If you find yourself in this space, you can do some work on refining your message or exploring if you can help this client on a different stage of their journey.

10. The Unfulfilled Coach

The second intersection is where your values, your clients' needs and what the client will pay for is considered but you feel you aren't fulfilling your potential as a coach, and this is because you aren't able to fully leverage your strengths in service of your clients.

This might be where you are holding back on fully embracing your intuition as a coach, or perhaps you're working with clients who also need support with skills you bring from your corporate career, such as sales or HR advice. Where you aren't fully leveraging your strengths, there are opportunities to create additional services to add to your portfolio of services so you can offer a broader range and make full use of your talents and experiences.

11. The Longing Coach

The third intersection is where your clients' needs and what they'll pay for are considered, so are your coaching strengths but you're neglecting your own values and what you enjoy.

Coaching in this space may feel joyless. You may have clients and be good at what you do, but you'll feel that the joy is missing from your work. For example, if you value progress and achievement, and find you are working with clients who enjoy taking small steps forward as opposed to giant leaps and massive progress, you may feel a longing to work with more ambitious clients. Or perhaps you value deep connection and find you are working with clients who are looking for coaching support with transactional goals, such as getting better at time management. You may long to work with clients who want to do deeper transformational change work.

If you find yourself here, it's a case of going back to consider your values and your clients' needs and refocus your efforts to bring all elements back together.

12. The Confused Coach

The fourth intersection is where what your clients will pay for is considered, so are your coaching strengths and values but the clients' needs are not considered. This is a confusing place to coach because you'll be appealing to clients who have clear goals, but there's a risk that those goals are misaligned to their values and needs. The danger here is that through coaching, the clients discover that they want different goals, and whilst they are delighted at having discovered their real needs through coaching, it's going to be hard for you to build your reputation as a coach for delivering consistent results.

An example here is where you have a core message that you help people to transition careers, but you don't talk about why. So, you attract clients with varying needs, some are doing it for more balance, others for freedom, perhaps even for more financial gain. So, when clients come to you for coaching and connect to those needs, some may discover that they don't want to transition at all, they just needed to learn how to put in place boundaries so they could better manage their time. If you'd been clear in your messaging that you help clients to create a better balance in life, you'd attract clients who recognise the need to do just that, and you can build a reputation for these results. Without considering the needs, you'll attract a variety of clients, which might be engaging for you, but makes it harder to build a reputation for consistent results.

The destination is to have all four quadrants fully considered so that you are clear on your ideal client and therefore the niche that you serve, which takes us to the last part of The Niche Map

13. Your Ideal Client and Niche

This is where the client is ready, willing, and able to invest in your services and you love serving their needs. You'll know when you have achieved your ideal client and niche when you are in absolute flow working with your clients. You'll enjoy the work, be good at it and know that the clients you're working with are a great fit for you and your services.

It may take time to completely tie down your niche and that's ok, enjoy the journey as you learn and grow.

Using The Niche Map

You may not be able to fully complete all areas of The Niche Map given that you are at the start of your journey so this is a resource that you can come back to time and time again as your experience grows and you get closer and closer to your goal. To help you take the first steps on your journey, make a start on thinking of defining your niche. You can use the questions below to guide you here:

1. What are your coaching strengths?
2. What do you most enjoy helping people with? How does this relate to your values?
3. What needs do you most want to help people fulfil? (The intangible results)
4. What are the tangible results that the people you want to work with are looking for?

Once you've fully completed these quadrants you can move on to consider the spaces in between.

1. Your Coaching Passion: How would you describe what you are most passionate about when it comes to coaching?
2. Your Coaching Mission: What do you feel called to help people with?
3. Your Core Message: What are the results that your clients can expect from working with you? Think about tangible and intangible results.

4. Your Unique Style: What makes your coaching unique?

Once you've answered all these questions, you'll have a good idea of area of coaching you want to work in. Now you need to add some detail. The final questions you need to answer to fully discover your niche and ideal client are:

1. Who does this client remind you of? Why?
2. Do you see yourself in this client? If so, when in your life were you this person? What was happening at the time? (If not you, then who?)
3. What role are they engaged in at the moment? How would they describe their professional self?
4. What's happening for them personally? How would they describe their personal life?
5. If you were searching for this client on LinkedIn, what job title would you be searching for and what industry would you find them in?

REFLECTION QUESTIONS

As we draw this chapter to a close, let's finish with some questions for you to reflect on to help you to start figuring out your coaching niche could be:

Who would you enjoy working with as a coach?

What problems would you like to support them with?

What results would you like to help them get?

186 • DECIDING TO COACH

CHAPTER SUMMARY

The key learning points in this chapter include:

1. Niching helps you to distinguish yourself in a crowded market. It's about talking directly to the people that you want to help. It doesn't mean that others won't get to work with you, they are likely to approach you anyway.
2. You can use the Niche Map to help you clarify your niche and messaging.
3. The Niche Map will help you to avoid common pitfalls that coaches can fall into.

SELLING

"Coaching is a process. It's how we help our clients with the goals or challenges they face. Most people aren't attracted to processes. They are attracted to results"

— *JO WHEATLEY & ZOE HAWKINS*

Once you have identified your likely niche, you can embrace the selling aspect of running a successful and sustainable coaching business. People buy solutions to problems. When you purchase anything, it's with a view to resolving a problem. When selling coaching you'll be focusing on the solution that you are providing to your ideal clients and helping them to understand how coaching enables the achievement of their needs. In this chapter, we're going to be talking about how to sell coaching ethically and in alignment with your values.

188 · DECIDING TO COACH

Coaching is a process. It's how we help our clients with the goals or challenges they face. Most people aren't attracted to processes. They are attracted to results. They want to know how what they are buying helps them to get better results, so when you're selling coaching you need to be able to talk to the pain points your client is experiencing and also their deepest desires - their aspirations. When it comes to coaching, both tangible and intangible results are important.

Tangible results are things like:

- Earning more money
- Getting promoted faster
- Growing your network
- Changing careers easily
- Delegating more effectively
- Resolving conflict in teams

Intangible results are things like:

- Greater confidence
- Having clarity
- Better balance in work and life
- Emotional stability
- More ease
- Greater fulfilment

Coaching is a significant investment of time, money and effort, and your prospective clients (whether it is an individual purchasing or organisation on behalf on an employee) may not be used to investing in this. Buying coaching services can be something people procrastinate about before deciding to take the plunge and invest. It's easy to 'not get around to' investing in a coach as there are always other things to invest in, seeking attention. There is often a trigger point or event that makes finding a coach more urgent – perhaps it's a conflict at work, or a particularly stressful meeting or project. Selling coaching successfully is about being seen in your client's world regularly so that they are thinking of you when they need you.

Your visibility is key here. Remember what we said in the communities chapters, "your clients have to know you exist for them to be able to work with you" and not only do they need to know you exist, they need to see you all the time. So as well as building your own communities, you can boost your visibility by being a guest in others. Some examples of this are:

- Guest podcasting
- Speaking in other people's groups and memberships as a guest expert
- Contributing to writing in other people's blogs or books
- Speaking at local networking groups or events
- Being a guest speaker at a conference

Activities like these boost your visibility and keep you in front and centre of your ideal client's mind. When your ideal clients see you in your communities, as well as others, there is a compound effect to your visibility, and the trust your prospective clients develop in you, as other people start talking about you too. It's important when doing this to look for opportunities and collaborations with people who have complimentary audiences, not where you are competing for the same ideal clients, and this is where you can get creative. If you know that your ideal clients are avid walkers, you could connect with people who hold walking groups and volunteer to host a talk in one of their groups. If you know your ideal clients are health conscious, you could research health podcasts and pitch to be a guest expert.

Another way to draw your clients' attention to your services is to launch them. Launching increases your visibility and ensures you are in your client's field of awareness. It's a way to build your brand, grow your email list and also add value to your prospective clients so they either want to start working with you, or plan to start working with you.

Launching is where you hold an event, or series of events, and share an offer for a service that you are selling off the back of that event. It's a way to give value to potential clients and give them a taster of what your services may be like. Launching is most commonly used for group programmes and courses, but it can also be an effective way to launch 1:1 services.

Let's explore three launch options and help you to get a feel for how you may like to launch your services:

1. A Challenge

A challenge is a typically a three or four day event where potential clients are tasked with a small activity to do each day. You may have seen these held in Facebook Groups, you can also host them live via video conferencing. Incorporating live elements are a way to boost engagement and very easy to do when you have a small audience.

Each day you would either host a live broadcast or post a pre-recorded video or post explaining what you invite your group members to do.

The purpose of the challenge is to help your prospective clients get ready for investing in your services, so if you know that one barrier that prospective clients face is not having clear goals to focus on, you would design a challenge that led them through bite size activities that resulted in them having clear goals by the end of it.

At the end of your challenge, you make an offer for challenge members to join you in one of your services. It can be a good idea to have people sign up for a masterclass at this point so that you have an audience to talk to who you know are interested in investing in your services. On the masterclass, you would share additional value and make your offer live on the class.

A challenge is a great way to launch if you are good at maintaining energy and bringing people together. It can be a lot of fun and a great way to build relationships with prospective clients. Whether people decide to purchase or not, you will be creating loyal fans who place you firmly on their radar and will probably recommend you to others.

2. A Masterclass

A masterclass, even without a challenge, can be a great way to launch. A masterclass is a live event where people register to join you to learn something from you. It's often held via a video conferencing system, such as zoom.

When you use a masterclass to launch, the topic needs to be of high value to your clients, something they would easily give their time up for. The idea of the masterclass is that it imparts knowledge or skills that your prospective clients are highly drawn to.

You would typically host a number of the same masterclasses, offering them at different times so that you can be sure your prospective clients can make one of the dates. Masterclasses tend to last between 60-90 minutes, are best run live and made interactive so that your attendees engage with you throughout the class, either using a chat function, or if your audience is smaller, inviting people to speak and share.

Towards the end of your masterclass, after you have delivered exceptional value to your attendees, you will transition into making an offer to them. This can be something natural like, 'if you have enjoyed our session today, you can continue your journey with me by joining me in a coaching relationship', and then you can go on to share all the details of your offer.

3. A Summit

A summit is an event held over a couple of days where you invite a number of guest speakers to share their knowledge and insight into an area of interest for your client. Summits can be held live via an online platform.

The benefit of a summit is to offer extraordinary value from a number of different perspectives. You take the role of host and can mention your offer or services throughout the summit sessions so you get a prolonged period of time to talk about what your offer. At the end of the summit, you can invite people for a 'wrap up' session and share key highlights, takeaways and of course, your offer.

Summits can be a great way to take some of the pressure and attention off yourself, as you share the stage with many people. The mutual value is that summit speakers get exposure to your audience, but you have to get the balance right. The whole idea of a launch is to share your offer and services and meet prospective clients, so make sure you design it in such a way that you manage to achieve this.

With all of these launch strategies, there are additional things that can enable people to buy with confidence. Creating a sense of urgency with your clients can help them to overcome procrastination and make the decision to invest, if that is what they want to do. Here are four effective ways that you can do this:

Offer Bonuses

You may choose to offer bonuses to the first few people that sign up to your coaching package, or to everyone that signs up in the first 24/48 hours.

A bonus is something of high value that you know your client's desire. Bonuses can come in different forms:

- Extra time with you
- PDF 'how to' guides
- Downloadable relaxation recordings
- A free book that supports their learning

You can be creative and design bonuses that you know your clients would love and enjoy.

Limit Capacity

As a coach, you do not have unlimited capacity. If you launch your coaching services you may end up with over 100 people registered for your launch event, so you will need to limit the number of clients you can take on. Limiting space creates urgency as some people will not want to miss out. It's important that you only do this if it is genuine for you and your business. Falsely limiting spaces and misleading clients about what is or isn't available is unethical.

Social Proof And Testimonials

People like to buy with confidence and one way we can offer that when selling coaching packages is through social proof and testimonials.

On a coaching training you will be working with 'practice clients', these clients will be your first testimonials of your work. Always ask your clients as you wrap up your coaching to provide you with a testimonial. You can make your request by email or use a survey to capture wider feedback about your work.

Social proof is where you share snapshots from messages or social media posts where you and your services are mentioned. This helps your prospective clients to see that others are investing in you and talking about you positively. Others results create a sense of "fear of missing out' and this can help clients to reach a decision to invest too.

Remember if you are sharing private information always check with your client first. As coaches, the trust and confidence your client has in you comes first.

Personal Outreach

Coaching is ultimately about relationships. When a client chooses to invest in your services they are entering a relationship of deep trust and connection. Therefore, personal outreach to clients, asking them if they have any questions or reflections about what they learned on during your launch event is a great way to build deeper relationships and explore the level of interest your prospective clients have in working with you. You can do this with voice notes or videos too.

Lastly, never under estimate the value of your network. Whilst there are many online activities you can do such as creating communities, guesting in other people's and launching your services online, the people you know and have relationships with will always be ready and willing to help you if you continue to nurture those relationships. Ex colleagues, peers in your current industry, people you went to school with and of course, your clients, will all support and recommend you, and often the more visible you are, the more opportunity they have to remember you and share you as a recommendation to their connections.

When you are starting out, this is likely to be the first place you will go to and we recommend to all our learners that they tell everyone in their network their plans and proactively ask for recommendations, referrals, even testimonials from when they worked together, as a way to get a foot up in business. Whilst this may feel unnatural to you, we know that most people are kind-hearted and want to help, they also enjoy hearing from you as many people will be inspired by your story. You simply have to lean into courage to put yourself out there and ask. It's what we did when we first started and we have never been out of work since the day our business began.

Like all things in business, you have to do what feels right for you and your clients and you get to experiment and discover what those things are. Make sure you also challenge yourself to move out of your comfort zone and do the things that feel stretchy too. Not everything will "feel easy" if it's ambitious.

REFLECTION QUESTIONS

As we draw this chapter to a close, let's finish with some questions for you to reflect on to help you consider your view of selling your coaching services:

What excites you about selling and launching coaching services?

Which of the launch options appeal to you the most?

CHAPTER SUMMARY

The key learning points in this chapter include:

1. When it comes to selling coaching you need to engage in activities that move coaching up your prospective clients 'to do' list.
2. You're never really selling coaching. You are selling a solution to a problem that your client has.
3. Launching your coaching services is a great way to draw attention to what you are selling and also a way to get your business off the ground.

MONEY MINDSET

> "Transitioning from a corporate career into business as a coach is going to challenge your mindset in ways that you haven't encountered before"
>
> — JO WHEATLEY & ZOE HAWKINS

Coaches support people to align their mindset to their goals and running your own coaching business requires a strong mindset. The first hurdle many new coaches face is getting comfortable with the idea of selling their coaching services and setting their prices. We know it's at this point that many coaches feel uncomfortable and resist putting themselves forward to work with paying clients. Overcoming the discomfort of pricing is a really important part of growing a successful and sustainable coaching business. Pricing is a decision that all coaches must take and review regularly. What will I charge, and how will I sell my services? These questions will lead you to meet your money mindset, so in this chapter, we'll help you with the practicalities of setting prices and what to do with your money mindset.

Setting prices can stop new coaches getting started. It's a big transition to move from being employed and receiving a wage to determining what you will charge others for your services. The reality is, that you can charge whatever feels right for your coaching services and when you start researching you'll see there are huge differences in what coaches charge.

There are two types of pricing models in the coaching industry. There's the model which charges by the hour for coaching sessions and the model which charges for the transformation. When charging by the hour, the coach is using a traditional model of pricing which involves working out what you want to earn, calculating total expenses and using this to work out an hourly rate.

Once you have your hourly rate, you'd need to check that this is aligned to what your client would pay and how it fits within the industry. Whether it's an individual paying or an organisation may impact this. Why the difference? It's to do with the perceived potential for impact.

The transformation pricing model focuses less on cost and more on value. It's where the coach is no longer charging for their time and instead charges for value that the results of the coaching bring. Transformation pricing is about demonstrating value through strong messaging that focuses on tangible and intangible results.

For example, if you are a coach who supports clients to grow their business, over time you can gain testimonial and references that demonstrate the typical growth experienced. Off the back of your results, you can then set your prices to align with the value you are generating for your clients. If you are a coach that helps clients to progress in their career and secure promotions, over time you can gather results that show the typical progression route of your clients and how their career progress has enabled them to increase their earnings. You can use these stories to demonstrate the tangible value of your coaching packages.

Many coaches start out by pricing their services by the hour and as they gain experience and reputation, slowly increase their prices and develop their messaging so they move into pricing for the transformation. The point here is that nothing is permanent, setting prices doesn't have to stop you, you can adjust your prices in line with your growth and what you are learning about business.

Another consideration you may like to reflect on when setting your prices is where you want to position yourself within your niche – or market. There are brands for everything, value brands and premium brands and everything in between. As a coach, you are essentially building a brand. The client you are talking to will come to understand why you do what you do, how you work and what results you deliver. This is your brand and it is down to you to design it and position yourself as you want to be seen. Your pricing needs to match your brand. If you decide that you want to become an Executive Coach, working with C-suite leaders on their strategic vision and wellbeing, you are likely to be looking at premium pricing. If you are not, there will be a misalignment and your services are likely to be disregarded as too cheap.

Likewise, if your branding looks unprofessional and your imagery is hazy, yet your prices are some of the highest in your niche, there will be a misalignment there too and so it is likely that you will lose work. When it comes to positioning, branding, visuals, messaging, pricing – it all matters, and so when building your business, this is something to spend time on and think about how your positioning and pricing aligns to your values and where you want to work in the market.

Setting prices and positioning your services is a mindset journey because you have to put a value on what you believe your work is worth and given that you are the one delivering the work, it can feel like you are putting a price on yourself. We have seen coaches literally recoil in horror at just the thought of pricing their services and making sales. The word selling often brings up memories and images of cold calling, pressurised sales tactics and pushy, unethical approaches. The good news is that this is not what selling coaching is about.

In the coaching industry, selling is being in service. It's about sharing solutions that your clients want and need. In reality, discomfort with selling is often not about the selling at all, it's about mindset. So, what is it about selling that creates discomfort in coaches?

We find three main blocks that can be at the source of this challenge for new coaches:

1. Worthiness – the extent to which you believe you are worthy
2. Rejection – fear of being rejected and a need to be liked
3. Money Mindset – the relationship you have with money

We'll explore each in turn.

Worthiness

We all have an intrinsic sense of our self worth. Stepping into business as a coach requires us to charge for our services and you have to put a financial figure against what your services are worth. It's at this point that we'll often misinterpret this to be what "we" are worth, because our services are an extension of who we are. Setting prices and charging for your services is likely to be outside of your comfort zone, so learning to tolerate some of that discomfort whilst you work through it, will be an important part of your journey.

New coaches can start by identifying and challenging the beliefs they hold about themselves and proactively work on developing a mindset that will support their growth as a coach. As you gain the skills to coach others through your coaching training, this is something you will learn to do for yourself and if you need extra support in this space you can also seek that from a coach yourself! We shared with you some tools to use to change limiting beliefs earlier in the book. You may want to turn back the pages to that section and work through the activities with your beliefs about selling coaching services.

Rejection

It's not often the selling that scares us. It's a fear of rejection. When someone says no to your services, there's every chance you'll feel it personally. It may trigger your inner critic "Oh my prices were too high, who am I to think that I could charge that much for my work?", "They don't think I'm good enough to be a coach and now everyone else knows it too". The need to be liked, accepted and belong is common to many people, it helps us to feel safe and is often a core part of our values.

When it comes to selling, we need to be able to stand in the confidence of knowing we are liked, accepted and belong, whether or not someone buys our services. This will be a new feeling or experience if you haven't done this before and many coaches naturally overcome this discomfort with time. If you find it challenging to move through that on your own, the good news is that you can be amongst a community of coaches who can help you with those challenges. Remember, you are resourceful and your mind is powerful. It is possible for you to work through these blocks and even be at ease with selling and enjoy the process! It can be helpful to budget for a coach yourself to support you as you set up and develop your business.

Money Mindset

We all have a relationship with money that will have been influenced by how we have been brought up. Here are a few examples:

- You have to work hard for money
- Money doesn't grow on trees
- Money is the root of all evil
- It's rude to talk about money
- You have to be careful with money

These beliefs can impact the decisions you make in your coaching business. Awareness is the first step and secondly, resolving the beliefs that are limiting you so you can achieve the goals you want to achieve in creating your successful and sustainable coaching business.

When we work in an employed role, we don't often question our relationship with money because it's someone else's money that is paying us. When it's our own money that pays our wage, it can bring up new emotions and unfamiliar sensations. Uncovering and working through your money stories will help you to cultivate a healthy relationship with money that will serve you in your new journey as a coach. Again, you can use the skills you gain through your coaching training to work on this yourself, or you can budget to work with a coach to support you on that journey.

As you continue to invest in your own wellbeing through coaching, you will find charging for your services becomes easier. Here are some ways to think about selling that may help you to engage with the idea with excitement and passion.

1. People buy from people, your main job is to build relationships
2. When you believe wholeheartedly in what you're selling, you know you're adding value
3. If you do a great job of talking about the value your services provide, you won't need to 'convince' people to buy from you
4. Your ideal clients have been looking for you and your services and need you to let them know you can support them
5. Selling is connecting
6. Selling is a conversation

REFLECTION QUESTIONS

As we draw this chapter to a close, let's finish with some questions for you to reflect on to help you consider your view of selling your coaching services:

What is your money story?

What will help you to set your process with confidence?

CHAPTER SUMMARY

The key learning points in this chapter include:

1. You can charge whatever you like for your coaching

206 • DECIDING TO COACH

services. It's a vast industry and there are enormous variances in what coaches charge for their coaching services.

2. There are two types of pricing models in the coaching industry.

SO WHAT NOW?

Here we are at the end of the final chapter, and in many ways, whilst this is the last chapter of our book, it is in fact, the beginning of your decision and the actions that will come from that. You started this journey with a decision to make, and through part one you've expanded your knowledge and awareness of what coaching is. You've taken a look inside of yourself to understand your strengths and values and how these align to coaching. You've also explored the beliefs you hold about making a decision to transition into coaching and how you'd need to align your identity to what you want and need. In doing so, you've also learnt how you can gain control over your emotions and use them as a powerful source of motivation and change, as well as setting goals that bring you closer to living in alignment with your values.

In part two, you connected with why deciding to coach is important to you, the reason you picked up book in the first place, and once you connected with that reason, we've shared with you how a successful and sustainable coaching business can be achieved. You've had the opportunity to read about and reflect on how to build your coaching business through community, how to build a coaching business with a portfolio of services, what activities you'd need to invest in and engage with when starting out, as well as where you might niche your coaching business

Notice how we start with mindset, and end with mindset. Everything in life comes down to the mindset you choose to have. You have everything you need now to make your decision, and really, you have two options: you can close this book and carry on mulling over your options, or you can choose to make changes, one small step at a time. You are a resourceful, tenacious and agile learner. You have all the resources within you that you need to make the changes in your life that will bring you into alignment with your strengths and values, or you can get them.

As you prepare to close this book, what are you choosing in your decision? Stay as you are? Or take steps to make change?

Here are a few small steps if you want to keep you moving in the direction of training to be a coach:

1. Come and find out which coaching course is right for you by completing our quiz at www. mycoachingcourse.com.
2. Speak to us about training to be coach by contacting us at info@igcompany.co.uk.
3. Tell your friends you've decided to make some important career changes and watch how they feel inspired by your courage.

Whatever your next steps, we believe in you.

Warmly,

Zoe and Jo

HOW WE CAN SUPPORT YOU

Thank you for taking the time to read our book and follow through each of the chapters. If you are drawn to the work we do and want to work with us, we'll outline below the different ways we invite you to do that:

Accredited Coaching Training

Our coaching training programmes are the heart beat of the work we do. It is our life's work to enable people to develop world class coaching skills to be able to create a positive legacy in the world through raising aspirations and everyday mental health. We offer coaching trainings at different levels to suit individual's needs. You can find out more about our coaching training programmes and coach CPD here:

https://www.igcompany.co.uk

We have a quiz that you can complete and it will tell you which coaching course is right for you:

www.mycoachingcourse.com

1:1 Coaching

We work with a limited number of 1:1 clients each year. You can find out about our 1:1 coaching programmes by visiting our individual websites.

www.jowheatley.com

www.zoe-hawkins.com

The Coaching Crowd Business Lounge

This is our paid membership to support coaches to set up a successful and sustainable coaching business. We have on online learning platform, as well as a community space with expert speakers and live Q&A's with us.

https://www.igcompany.co.uk/lounge

Coaching Crowd

This is our free Facebook group for people interested in training to be a coach or developing as a coach. We share resources and have an open forum to ask any questions about coaching.

https://www.facebook.com/groups/TheCoachingCrowd

ACKNOWLEDGMENTS

This book has been forming since the day we were both born and therefore we would like to take the opportunity to recognise some key people who have influenced us in our lives and are therefore somewhat included in the DNA of this book. Our teachers have included our parents, our friends, our coaching trainers, our children and our partners.

Particular thanks to our parents, partners and children who have enabled us to spend hours writing and drafting this book and talking it through. You are all part of our extended team.

We'd like to thank all the coaching trainees who have put their trust in us to enable them to connect with their inner coach and support them with new perspectives, tools and enable them to do incredible work. Special thanks to those who chose us in the early days, without whom, we may never have got to this point.

Thanks also to our coaching supervisors who have held safe spaces for us to develop and grow as coaches and CEOs of a coaching business.

We'd like to thank Authors & Co for guiding us through the stages to get published.

REFERENCING

2. WHAT IS COACHING?

1. ICF website: https://coachingfederation.org/faqs
2. EMCC Global Competence Framework V2
3. EMCC Global Competence Framework V2